'It was a real pleasure to read Dr
Based Cognitive Behaviour Therap
Self. Professor Wong is a master
and a Fellow of the Academy o
as a practicing social worker a
comprehensive and internation

nitive behavior therapy and combines this with the best of strength-based
approaches to psychotherapy. This volume is a empirically-based treatment
manual which lays out a sophisticated methodology solidly based on intervention research conducted by the author and others. Having already written
17 books and treatment manuals, this newest contribution by Dr. Wong to
the research-supported treatment literature is a compendium of practical and
effective approaches to the assessment and treatment of clients with a wide
array of mental health problems and difficulties in everyday living. I cannot
commend this book highly enough to psychotherapists wishing to learn about
a genuinely effective approach to treatment.'

– *Bruce A. Thyer,*
Distinguished Research Professor, College of Social Work, Florida State University, USA

'The key to successful application of strength-based cognitive-behaviour therapy on mental health recovery hinges on how well professionals such as social
workers, counsellors, and other health care professionals are equipped with
relevant theoretical knowledge and competence using the requisite intervention tools and skills, as well as are practicing in an environment that facilitates a recovery-oriented approach to care. Professor Daniel Wong from the
University of Hong Kong, his team and agency colleagues from Hong Kong
Baptist Oi Kwan Social Services have ingeniously integrated the recovery concept, strengths perspective, and cognitive-behavioural therapy in developing
a practice model which infuses autonomy, hope, meaning, purpose, and social
connectedness in the lives of people with mental illness. Using a metaphor
"from trapped self to liberated self," this book is a consolidation of Professor
Wong and his team's practice wisdom and insights on this innovative approach
on mental health recovery. The case illustrations give a detailed, comprehensive and easy-to-understand analysis of the different phases and techniques
involved in the process of recovery. This book is exceedingly readable, yet
inspiring; and will be an invaluable resource for the helping professionals.'

– *Yin-Ling Irene Wong,*
Associate Professor and Interim Associate Dean for Global Studies
at the School of Social Policy and Practice, University of Pennsylvania, USA

'This book draws on recent work done on the application of a person's
strengths to psychotherapy. It will not only appeal to CBT therapists, but also
to those wishing to explore the relevance of CBT to coaching'

– *Windy Dryden,*
Emeritus Professor of Psychotherapeutic Studies, Goldsmiths University of London, UK

A Strength-Based Cognitive Behaviour Therapy Approach to Recovery

This is the first practice-oriented book to provide professionals with a clear and practical guide in delivering strength-based recovery-oriented CBT intervention. Essentially, strength-based CBT moves away from a deficit and rehabilitation model and offers a person with mental illness a sense of renewed hope and meaning of life. With plenty of case illustrations, the book integrates the recovery model and cognitive-behaviour approaches and provides readers with a theoretical understanding of the recovery process and how various cognitive-behaviour strategies can be skilfully applied to different stages of the recovery process. It is written for professionals such as psychiatrists, psychologists, social workers, occupational therapists, and nurses in the mental health fields. Step-by-step illustrations of the use of the various cognitive behavioural strategies and worksheets are provided throughout the book.

Daniel Fu Keung Wong is a social work academic and a clinical psychologist. His research team has been actively conducting research in mental health practice, and he is a pioneer in indigenizing the application of cognitive behaviour therapy (CBT) for Chinese people with depression, anxiety problems, chronic illnesses, gambling problems, and drug addictions. Regarding mental health issues, Professor Wong and his team have conducted numerous studies on mental health literacy of Chinese people in Hong Kong, China, Taiwan and Australia, and on mental health first aid for Chinese people in Hong Kong and Australia. He has written more than 100 academic papers and 15 books and professional manuals. Professor Wong and his colleagues established the Institute of Cognitive Therapy in Hong Kong and Centre for Holistic Health in Melbourne, Australia, to provide training for mental health professionals and promote better mental health among Chinese populations. His research interests include CBT, evidence-based practice in mental health, mental health promotion, mental health literacy, and mental health issues among migrants. Professor Wong has received numerous awards such as The Fulbright Fellowship, University of Hong Kong and Faculty of Social Sciences Outstanding Teaching Awards, Universitas 21 Fellowship, and Fellow of Academy of Cognitive Therapy.

Rose Wai Man Yu is a registered social worker with more than ten years of experience in the mental health field in Hong Kong, Canada, and China. She has worked with Professor Wong to prepare training materials and to write a book on cognitive behaviour therapy (CBT).

Viola Yuk Ching Chan is a social worker who has worked in mental health service for over 30 years. She has experience in providing clinical counselling and therapeutic groups, and supervising and training frontline social workers in various mental health service settings. Her main interest is application of cognitive behaviour therapy on treating different mental illnesses including depression, anxiety, and psychosis.

A Strength–Based Cognitive Behaviour Therapy Approach to Recovery

From Trapped to Liberated Self

Daniel Fu Keung Wong,
Rose Wai Man Yu and
Viola Yuk Ching Chan

Routledge
Taylor & Francis Group

LONDON AND NEW YORK

First published 2020
by Routledge
2 Park Square, Milton Park, Abingdon, Oxon OX14 4RN

and by Routledge
52 Vanderbilt Avenue, New York, NY 10017

Routledge is an imprint of the Taylor & Francis Group, an informa business

British Library Cataloguing in Publication Data
A catalogue record for this book is available from the British Library

Library of Congress Cataloguing in Publication Data
Names: Wong, Daniel Fu Keung, author. | Yu, Rose Wai Man, author. | Chan, Viola Yuk Ching, author.
Title: A strength-based CBT approach to recovery : from trapped to liberated self / Daniel Wong Fu Keung, Rose Yu Wai Man and Viola Chan Yuk Ching.
Description: Milton Park, Abingdon, Oxon ; New York, NY : Routledge, 2020. | Includes bibliographical references and index.
Identifiers: LCCN 2019012209| ISBN 9780367190910 (hardback) | ISBN 9780367190927 (pbk.) | ISBN 9780429200328 (e-book)
Subjects: LCSH: Mental illness—Treatment. | Cognitive therapy. | Psychotherapy.
Classification: LCC RC475 .W66 2020 | DDC 616.89/1425—dc23
LC record available at https://lccn.loc.gov/2019012209

ISBN: 978-0-367-19091-0 (hbk)
ISBN: 978-0-367-19092-7 (pbk)
ISBN: 978-0-429-20032-8 (ebk)

Typeset in Bembo Std
by Cenveo® Publisher Services

Contents

Preface

People recovering from mental illness face many challenges in life, including public stigma and discrimination, and are confined to a trapped self, which is characterized by passivity and a lack of hope and purpose in life. A strength-based cognitive behaviour therapy (SBCBT) approach aims to facilitate a person in recovery to identify his/her own personal goals and to use his/her strengths and resources to build his/her road to mental health recovery. Unfortunately, there is a scarcity of literature concerning the concept of recovery and the implementation of a strength-based approach for working with Chinese people in recovery. In view of these, Professor Daniel Fu Keung Wong and the staff of Baptist Oi Kwan Social Services have jointly developed this innovative SBCBT approach on mental health recovery. The three components in the project were: (1) training of professionals in SBCBT, (2) monthly supervision, and (3) evaluation.

In the beginning, all social workers participating in this project had to undergo a five-day training to understand and to learn to apply cognitive behaviour therapy (CBT) concepts in working with people recovering from mental illness. Following the training, the participating colleagues began to provide SBCBT to their clients and received monthly supervision for the entire period of implementation. In the beginning, colleagues were skeptical about the practicality of applying the integrated CBT and recovery model in working with people recovering from mental illness. Through the 18 months of practice experience, colleagues acquired a good command of the use of SBCBT, and we hope to document this experience and share our practice wisdom with other professionals who are interested in applying SBCBT to people recovering from mental illness.

This book is suitable for professionals such as social workers, counselors, and other health care professionals. Chapter 1 lays out the conceptual framework, including the concept and principles of recovery, and the roles of professionals in the recovery process. It also delineates the SBCBT model on mental health recovery. Chapter 2 documents two cases that illustrate the processes and skills involved in SBCBT on mental health recovery. From Chapter 3 to Chapter 9, we introduce the seven phases of the SBCBT process of mental health recovery, and highlight, with case examples, how certain stage-specific SBCBT strategies can be played out in the various processes. Chapter 10 covers colleagues' reflections on the use of the SBCBT model, and Chapter 11 describes the results of the clinical outcome of the SBCBT interventions on clients who participated in the process.

We want here to offer our sincere thanks to all our clients who are in this book, whose names have been anonymized, for allowing us to share their experiences. We also want to thank all colleagues who dedicated their time and trust in going through the various processes of the project. Together, we have implemented a truly academic–professional–client collaborative effort in developing an intervention model that addresses certain needs of individuals in our society.

Professor Daniel Fu Keung Wong
Dr. Rose Wai Man Yu
Miss Viola Yuk Ching Chan

1 Conceptual foundations of strength-based cognitive behaviour therapy in mental health recovery

Introduction

People who have problems in living are essentially stuck in the trapped self. This trapped self is characterized by: (1) being passive, (2) a lack purpose and direction in life, (3) low self-esteem, (4) feelings of being controlled by the social environment, and (5) a sense of social isolation. By contrast, the liberated self manifests the following characteristics: (1) being active, (2) having a purposeful and meaningful life, (3) having hopes in life, (4) being autonomous and self-fulfilling, and (5) enjoying good social and interpersonal relationships. The major purpose of strength-based cognitive behaviour therapy (SBCBT) is to facilitate an individual to move from a state of trapped self to a state of liberated self. In the seven phases of our SBCBT process, the worker adopts a strength perspective and facilitates the person to instil motivation for change, identify and set meaningful life goals for him/herself, develop action plans and strategies, identify and utilize personal strengths and external resources to fulfil life goals, identify and overcome obstructions, and, finally, reach his/her life goals (see Figure 1.1). In this chapter, we describe the SBCBT model in detail and illustrate how it can be applied in working with people recovering from mental illnesses. To begin, let's review the concepts of recovery and its importance in the field of mental health and mental illness.

Recovery — concepts, principles, and role of mental health workers

The concept of rehabilitation

Rehabilitation services for people with mental illness were first developed in the early 1950s. The term *rehabilitation* is defined as a process by which a person with a mental illness is helped to re-integrate into the community with the goal of returning to a 'normal' life. According to Wing (1981), factors affecting the severity of psychiatric disabilities fall mainly into three groups: (1) psychiatric impairments resulting from the illness (e.g., residual symptoms such

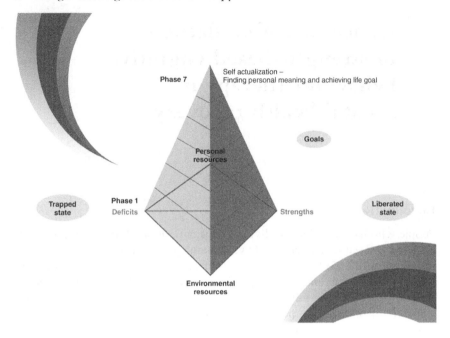

Phase 7

Self actualization –
Finding personal meaning and achieving life goal

Goals

Personal
resources

Trapped
state

Phase 1
Deficits

Strengths

Liberated
state

Environmental
resources

Figure 1.1 Towards an understanding of the conceptual foundation of strength-based cognitive behaviour therapy on recovery.

as hallucinations and delusions); (2) social disadvantages (e.g., social stigma attached to the psychiatric illness); and (3) individual psychological barriers (e.g., low self-esteem). All these factors could affect a person's level of social disablement, influencing his/her progress during the rehabilitation process. In Hong Kong, community-based psychiatric services have been established to provide rehabilitation services to minimize the extent of disablement suffered by people with mental illness, and to maximize this population's abilities to achieve community integration. The concept of rehabilitation assumes that a person with mental illness has certain deficits that may not be fully recovered, and the ultimate goal of rehabilitation is to optimize the person's personal and social functioning. In short, rehabilitation services focus on minimizing the deficits mental illness brings to an individual.

The concept of recovery

In contrast, the concept of *recovery* assumes that an individual with mental illness has strengths and resources that can be developed to build a meaningful and fulfilling life irrespective of the severity of his/her disablement. Indeed, the illness itself is only a part of the person's being, and the disablement resulting from one's mental illness may have little impact on or relevance to his/her overall happiness and satisfaction in life. Rather than focusing on an individual's deficits (as the concept of rehabilitation entails), the concept of recovery emphasizes the importance of helping the individual to identify and develop his/her strengths and interests so that he/she can lead a fulfilling, meaningful life.

This concept does not deny the need to learn ways of managing both the symptoms of mental illness and their negative impacts such as social discrimination. The concept emphasizes facilitating the individual with mental illness to develop his/her potential, seek personal growth, and pursue happiness in life. For example, a person with severe residual auditory hallucinations, who could not hold a paid job and felt inferior and useless to others, was encouraged by the worker to develop and make use of his artistic talent in making handicrafts. He was able to make lovely and practical handicrafts and sold them in various handicraft shops run by a non-government organization. Consequently, he accepted his state of unemployment, he felt satisfied with his renewed interest in making handicrafts, and he met new friends whom he would never have attempted to meet before. His auditory hallucinations were still affecting his daily functioning, but they did not hinder him from continuing to find meaning and fulfilment in making handicrafts.

Various scholars have defined the concept of recovery slightly differently. Anthony (1993) points out that having a mental illness is a life-changing process. During recovery, changes may appear in the attitudes, values, life goals, and roles of the person with mental illness. Despite the limitations posed by the illness, it is possible for the person with mental illness to be highly autonomous in finding his/her purpose in life. As the recovery process is uniquely individualized, the person with mental illness needs to identify and utilize his/her own internal and external resources to achieve his/her personal goals and aspirations. SAMHSA (2005) also considers recovery a process that can bring positive changes in the person's physical, psychological, and emotional well-being. A person in recovery is self-directed and would optimize his/her potentials purposefully and strategically. There are many similarities in the above two conceptualizations of recovery. Both consider recovery a process through which an individual can explore his/her internal strengths, interests, and goals, and work towards fulfilling those goals and achieving meaning in life. Second, the concept of recovery also acknowledges the limitations mental illnesses may place on the individual. In essence, whether the person can achieve his/her goals depends on how well he/she can minimize the deficits he/she faces and maximize his/her personal strengths and external resources.

Factors contributing to the state of trapped self

Why do people with problems of living get stuck in their states of trapped self? What barriers prevent them from liberating themselves from that trapped state? In the context of recovering from mental illness, these barriers can be summarized into the aspects discussed in this section.

Psychiatric disablement resulting from the severity of mental illness

As mentioned above, J. K. Wing (1981) identified three groups of factors affecting the severity of disability due to mental illness: (1) psychiatric impairments directly related to the mental illness, (2) social disadvantages resulting from the illness, and (3) personal psychological barriers. These factors contribute to keeping the individual with mental illness in a state of trapped self. Concerning psychiatric impairments, the more severe the illness (e.g., positive and negative symptoms), the more confined the person is in the trapped state. For example, a person with mental illness who is having difficulty concentrating and is underperforming at work because of frequent auditory/visual hallucinations, and is worrying about being harmed by others would have a multitude of problems re-integrating into the workforce. He/she may also be perceived as unproductive and can self-stigmatize oneself as being useless. Together, all of these factors keep the person in passivity, low self-esteem, and social isolation. Another example is a person with mental illness manifesting frequent unusual behaviours such as self-muttering may scare people away. Under such circumstances, it is likely that this person will be seen as strange and even dangerous, and would be kept at a distance. On the other hand, the person him/herself may perceive others' actions as unwelcoming and even hostile, resulting in social withdrawal and social isolation. The above two cases illustrate how people with mental illness can be stuck in the trapped self as a result of the severity of their psychiatric illnesses.

Not knowing one's own personal strengths and weaknesses

When a person with mental illness is unaware of his/her own strengths and weaknesses, he/she may not be motivated to make changes. In addition, a lack of understanding of one's strengths denies the person the opportunity to make use of his/her own internal and external resources to manage his/her life difficulties. In short, without a full recognition of one's strengths and weaknesses, the person is unable to enhance his/her strengths and minimize the weaknesses, and thus remains in the trapped self.

Dysfunctional response pattern to everyday life stresses

The negative response patterns to daily life stresses manifested by some people with mental illness can serve as another factor contributing to a person's confinement in the state of trapped self. All of us tend to respond with certain patterns towards life stresses, positive or not. For example, when trying something new, a person with a strong tendency to engage in negative self-talk will automatically think, 'I am incapable. I don't want to try'. Eventually, the readiness to try anything new diminishes. In this circumstance, others may feel annoyed and angry, and may not give him/her another chance.

Consequently, the person will end up feeling more frustrated and suffer a further loss of confidence. Another example is that, if a person with mental illness has difficulty controlling his/her negative emotions, when he/she encounters life difficulties, he/she may become highly emotional and express negative emotions immediately and in a destructive manner. This response pattern may be worrisome and scary for people around him/her. On the other hand, this person may experience a rejection and avoidance from his/her peers and family members. A vicious cycle is thus formed and the person is trapped in his/her own dysfunctional cognitive, behavioural, and emotional response patterns. The more deeply entrenched the dysfunctional response pattern is in the person, the more he/she is stuck in his/her trapped self.

Family factors

Family plays a significant role in the recovery process of a person with mental illness. The impacts can be positive or negative. On the positive side, family members can offer encouragement and provide support to the person with mental illness in his/her recovery process. However, negative emotions or verbal criticisms by family members can affect the confidence and sense of hope of the person with mental illness. Family members who are overly involved in the recovery process of the person with mental illness may sabotage the person's rights to self-determination, minimizing his/her self-confidence and capabilities to lead a meaningful and fulfilling life. In this family environment, some people with mental illness may learn to give up their rights to take charge and make choices, and play only a passive role in their own recovery processes. On the other hand, some family members harbour high expectations towards the person with mental illness such as insisting that the person with mental illness get back into the workforce and resume former activities soon after discharge from the hospital. When these expectations are not met, the family members may express disappointment and criticism towards the person with the illness. These negative attitudes and criticism will invariably affect the confidence of the person with mental illness, keeping him/her mired in the trapped self. In addition, other family members may simply give up on the person, and do not expect anything from him/her. Consequently, he/she may become more pessimistic in the road to recovery. To conclude, family members' over-involvement, negative criticism, and/or hostility can affect the active participation of the person with mental illness in his/her recovery process, keeping him/her in the undesirable state of trapped self.

Interpersonal relationship

Interpersonal relationship is another factor contributing to a person's continued entrapment in the trapped self. Similar to family members, friends who are important to the person with mental illness can also become overly involved, overly critical, or apathetic, affecting his/her level of social and occupational participation. On the other hand, a person with mental illness him/herself may also contribute to these negative aspects in interpersonal relationships. For example, if the person self-perceives that his/her friends, colleagues, or employers relate to him/her negatively because of his/her mental illness, he/she may avoid having social contacts or adopt a hostile attitude towards the others. Consequently, a vicious cycle of adverse interpersonal relationship may occur, keeping the person in a state of trapped self.

Environmentally induced dependency

Traditional mental health service systems generally adopt a medical model where the intervention plan for the person with mental illness is formulated under the lead of the medical professionals. The service recipient's level of participation is low and the recipient lacks the opportunity to make choices. Under these circumstances, the person with mental illness has to adapt to the environment instead of having his/her needs met flexibly by the environment. The needs and preferences of the person with mental illness are not given due consideration and he/she is not empowered to take charge and make his/her own choices in the recovery process. Under this medical-dominant approach, the capacity of the person with mental illness cannot be fully realized and he/she remains in the state of trapped self.

The previous discussion makes clear that under some or all of the stated conditions, the person with mental illness is gradually shaped into a state of trapped self. The self that is capable of taking charge and making choices is not liberated. The individual becomes passive without any life goal and lacks a purposeful and meaningful life. The so-called objectives for rehabilitation are set by the 'experts', and shaped by societal expectations and people around them. Not surprisingly, such a person becomes low in self-esteem, feels powerless, and is not able to exercise his/her own choice. He/she always feels controlled and alienated from the society. Incidentally, these feelings may also be felt among family members of the person with mental illness. On the contrary, under the recovery movement, the recovering person is facilitated to develop his/her life goals, hopes, and life meaning; he/she takes initiative to make plans in life and to achieve his/her goals and expectations. In addition, the person feels that he/she is part of the community and has a good relationship with others in the community. In short, the concept of recovery provides a perspective and a direction for transitioning a person with mental illness from a state of trapped self to that of the liberated self.

Six principles of the strength-based recovery model

The Department of Health of the Australian Government (2010) has proposed six principles to guide all psychiatric services in providing recovery-oriented mental health practices. The core themes in these principles revolve around providing a person with mental illness with hope, facilitating a better understanding of his/her capacity and impairment, developing a more active lifestyle, creating opportunities to take charge of one's life, and making choices about what he/she is interested in; and in the course of recovery, the person with mental illness achieves his/her life goals and life meaning. This governmental body also asserts that recovery does not imply that the person is symptom-free; it simply suggests that instead of focusing on treating symptoms, recovery-oriented services aim at increasing the motivation and autonomy of a person with mental illness.

The six principles are:

1   *Uniqueness of the individual*
    Mentally healthy or not, everyone is unique with personal preferences and strengths. For people recovering from mental illness, the recovery process involves facilitating these individuals to explore and fulfil their own unique values, interests, and goals in life. It is clearly stated that each individual's pathway to recovery is different and should be respected. Moreover, the objective of any recovery-oriented services is to empower the person to take charge of his/her recovery process, as he/she is the most significant agent of change.

2   *The individual's right to choices*
    Recovery-oriented services enable the recovering person to have his/her own choice in deciding the plan and the pace of recovery. The role of the worker is to work with the recovering person to explore his/her options and to encourage him/her to make appropriate choices. The worker provides guidance so that a balance between the right to make choices and public interest is well considered. For example, an individual who is mentally unwell at a certain period of time but insists on staying in the community instead of going to the hospital may need to be helped to weigh the potential risks and benefits of his/her actions to self and to the community. The worker should encourage the client to become a responsible member of the community while supporting the person to fulfil his/her choice.

3   *Upholding the rights of the individual*
    Regardless of one's mental health status, we are all members of the community. Each one of us has the right to receive community services and to do things according to our wishes. However, during the recovery process, the rights of many recovering persons are not protected. Some people are not even aware of those rights, let alone advocating for themselves. Recovery-oriented services advocate that a recovering person should be given full knowledge of his/her own rights in different facets of his/her life, such as in family relationships, the workplace, and so on. Workers should help the individual to stand up for him/herself. As such, the role of the worker is to listen to the needs of the recovering person and help him/her to protect and exercise his/her rights.

4   *Dignity and respect*

Recovery-oriented services aim to raise the awareness of the recovering person of his/her identity as a respectable and dignified member of the community. This awareness brings self-respect. It is common for people with mental disorders to feel stigmatized, discriminated against, ridiculed, and a low sense of dignity. Some might even be unable to function socially (e.g., getting a job) because of this negative sense of self. The feeling of not being respected may also result in self-stigmatization. He/she may simply think: 'I can't blame others for not respecting me because I am mentally ill and unproductive'. This self-labelling mechanism further reinforces the labelling effect, and, in turn, increases the feeling of not being respected.

Therefore, in recovery-oriented practices, the recovering person is encouraged to identify his/her own self-worth and be proud of his/her status as an individual in the society. In addition, recovery-oriented practices should aim to promote positive images of people with mental illness in the community.

5   *Partnership*

From a conventional rehabilitation perspective, people with mental illness are service users who receive assistance and services from service providers who are considered mental health experts. From a recovery-oriented perspective, the recovering person is the key participant in the process. His/her family members, friends, as well as service providers are all partners working together to help the person to get the services he/she wants and to achieve his/her goals during the recovery process. Under the rehabilitation model, the service providers are experts with the knowledge to assess the needs and to formulate intervention plans for the person with mental illness. In contrast, the recovery-oriented model proposes that the intervention plan is client-driven. The person with mental illness, instead of professionals, takes charge in deciding his/her needs. The role of a professional is to assist the recovering person in realizing what he/she wants to achieve.

6   *Evaluation*

The recovery-oriented model emphasizes the need to conduct ongoing evaluation throughout the recovery process. The intervention plan can then be constantly adjusted and/or enhanced to meet the needs of the recovering person. In the rehabilitation model, it is not uncommon to find that services are planned according to the subjective assessment of the providers and that little attention is paid to adjust to the dynamic changes in the needs of the person with mental illness in the changing social environments. Under the recovery model, the worker needs to constantly help the person evaluate the processes, identify successes and obstacles, and develop strategies to overcome the obstacles to goal attainment in the recovery process.

A brief overview of the recovery concept in different countries

There are many similarities in the implementation of the recovery concept across various countries and regions despite differences in the societal contexts in which the recovery concepts are used. In the United States and in Canada, for example, the New Freedom Commission on Mental Health (2003) has stated the intention to transform its traditional rehabilitation services to recovery services. The American Psychiatric Association (Hogan & Arrendondo, 2003) has also highlighted the importance of the recovery concept in psychiatric service provision, and advocates to promote recovery concepts at different levels of government and service. In addition, it suggests that training is important and should be provided to staff and peer supporters so that they can support their peers with mental illness (i.e., peer-to-peer support, peer-to-peer counselling).

In Australia and New Zealand, the adoption of the recovery concepts is included as part of the government policy in the provision of mental health services (O'Hagan, 2004; National Mental Health Plan, 2016). Professional mental health service providers are required to have knowledge of the recovery concepts and possess the necessary skills in implementing the recovery models.

In England and Ireland, the National Institute of Mental Health in England (2005) acknowledges the critical role of the recovery concepts in the provision of mental health services, and that the recovery concepts should also be adopted for public education. In Scotland, organizations such as the Scottish Recovery Network (Jacobson & Greenley, 2001) are also committed to the promotion of the recovery concepts for working with people with mental illness.

In sum, the recovery concepts are now widely adopted across countries and regions, although the expression of recovery concepts may differ from one place to another.

The roles of a mental health worker under the recovery model

Under the recovery concept, service providers have five roles:

Strengths assessor: The worker assesses the needs, interests, and life goals of a recovering person. At the same time, assessment should also be made to understand the internal and external resources of the person with mental illness. Furthermore, assessment should be a continuous process with the purpose of adjusting the intervention plan according to the needs of the person.

Goal development and attainment facilitator: The worker assists the recovering person in formulating his/her recovery action plan, and motivates and encourages him/her to follow through with the plan and achieve his/her goals.

Action plan moderator: The worker assists the recovering person in identifying the internal or external barriers to achieving his/her goals. The worker also works with the recovering person to explore problem-solving strategies to minimize the undesirable obstacles.

Human rights protector: Recovery-based principles value the rights and dignity of the recovering person. For various reasons, some recovering persons may not be capable of protecting their own rights and dignity. The worker should advocate on his/her client's behalf to safeguard his/her rights. At the same time, the worker has to educate the recovery person in understanding what rights he/she has and encourage him/her to exercise those rights.

Service broker: The worker acts as a bridge to facilitate the development of social support networks between the recovering person and his/her peers, friends, and professionals (e.g., medical care professionals) and coordinates different service units to ensure consistency in work plans and to minimize barriers. The worker also works with non-professionals in the social network of the recovering person to create an environment that is conducive to achieving his/her goals.

Strength-based cognitive behaviour approach for people recovering from mental illness

The meaning of strengths in recovery

There are many definitions of *strengths*. According to Jones-Smith (2014), strengths may be defined as attributes or traits that help a person cope with life or make life more fulfilling for oneself and others. These include at least 11 categories: (1) wisdom; (2) emotional strengths; (3) character strengths (e.g., courage); (4) creative strengths; (5) relational and nurturing strengths; (6) educational strengths; (7) analytical and cognitive strengths; (8) economic and financial strengths; (9) social support strengths; (10) survival skills; and (11) kinaesthetic and physical. When a person is aware of the presence of some or all of these attributes in him/herself, he/she can tap into these attributes to develop a more meaningful and satisfying life. The identification and utilization of these strengths consist of a process that is both culture- and context-specific (Jones-Smith, 2014). Our strengths convey to us what we value in life, what we have spent our time on, our preferences for the manner in which we engage our environment, and what we do well in life. Based on a resilience framework, Padesky and Mooney (2012) define strengths as strategies, beliefs, and personal assets that can promote the positive quality one is trying to build (e.g., resilience). The highlighted attributes include: (1) good health and easy temperament, (2) secure attachment and trust in others, (3) interpersonal competence, (4) cognitive competence, (5) emotional competence, (6) the ability and opportunity to contribute to others, and (7) meaning in life.

There are a great deal of similarities in the definitions of strength proposed by various scholars and practitioners. First, strengths are attributes that are present in an individual that can be used to build up a person. Second, the outcome of the utilization of one's strengths is idiosyncratic and depends on the objective set by the individual. It can include practical outcomes (e.g., getting a degree or certificate), psychological outcomes (e.g., self-actualization and meaning in life), and spiritual outcomes (e.g., spiritual revival). Third, strengths are applied in everyday life domains (i.e., including problems areas) that are perceived as areas with potentials for growth. Lastly, strengths cover both internal and external resources (i.e., including interpersonal resources).

In the mental health recovery process, the worker who adopts a strength-based approach would explore the client's strengths during the earlier stage of the process and would facilitate the client to utilize his/her internal and external resources to achieve his/her desired goals. Strengths can also be used to overcome the obstructions hindering goal attainment.

Integrating strength-based and cognitive-behaviour approaches

Theoretical consideration

As mentioned before, the strength-based approach emphasizes the exploration and utilization of personal strengths and external resources of the recovering person rather than focusing on the problem of the individual. Ironically, CBT has traditionally and conventionally been perceived as a problem-oriented approach, focusing on a client's problems and deficits. How can these two seemingly divergent approaches be meaningfully reconciled? In the literature, Padesky and Mooney (2012) have put forward a theoretical framework for their strength-based cognitive-behaviour approach. Based on a resilience perspective, they propose a four-step SBCBT model, which includes (1) search for strengths, (2) construct a personal model of resilience (PMR), (3) apply the PMR to areas of life difficulty, and (4) practice resilience. Essentially, it follows similar rationales and directions of intervention found in any strength-based intervention model: developing goals, searching for strengths, and helping the person to use strengths to work through his/her areas of life difficulty.

However, a number of critical issues in the Padesky and Mooney model require attention. First, there is a need to define more clearly what 'strengths' means in a strength-based intervention approach. In the Padesky and Mooney model, 'strengths' appears to be defined as personal and interpersonal resources (e.g., Davis, 1999, cited in Padesky and Mooney, 2012, p. 284). However, as suggested by Jones-Smith (2014), 'strengths' can be defined more broadly to encompass both internal strengths and external resources. The Jones-Smith definition has implications for a broader and a more comprehensive scope of assessment. (For more information, see our proposed assessment tool in later chapters.) Second, while there is no dispute over the emphasis on a search and development of strengths of an individual in a strength-based intervention process, the full expression of strengths can be possible only when certain conditions exist (e.g., a full recognition of a person's self-determination). In this regard, there is a need to deliberate the principles and conditions behind a SBCBT approach in intervention. Third, there is a lack of an emphasis on attention towards problems/obstacles in the Padesky and Mooney model because, as they suggest, 'by choosing to search within relatively untroubled areas of a person's life, the strengths discovered are more likely to be adaptive and not linked to cognitive distortions or maladaptive behaviours' (Padesky & Mooney, 2012, p. 285) and that 'people are generally more likely to hold distorted beliefs and maladaptive behaviour patterns in areas of difficulty than they do in areas where things go well in their life' (Padesky & Mooney, 2012, p. 285). What is at issue here is whether one can totally disregard the presence and influence of 'distorted beliefs and maladaptive behaviour patterns' (or any other deficits) that are inevitably and fundamentally affecting one's attainment of goals. Using recovery in mental illness as an example, the recovery process mainly involves developing a person's strengths to establish a meaningful life, but it is also necessary to facilitate the person to understand and deal with his/her internal deficits and external limitations affecting his/her recovery. 'Obstacles' and their successful resolution are part of the process of recovery and due attention must be paid towards them. In our SBCBT model, 'obstacles' and their successful resolution constitute an important stage of the seven-phase recovery process.

In this regard, conventional CBT provides a good theoretical framework with practical strategies for the person to understand and deal with his or her dysfunctional response patterns and beliefs, which act as obstacles to his/her goal attainment. Indeed, CBT intervention studies conducted by Grant et al (2012, 2017) reveal that dysfunctional (i.e., self-defeatist and asocial) beliefs, in conjunction with neurocognitive impairment, impeded functioning among people with schizophrenia, and that the SBCBT approach was able to reduce symptoms and improve overall functioning of people with schizophrenia. For example, workers using SBCBT can help the person in recovery understand his/her personal obstacles by facilitating him/her to identify his/her pattern of dysfunctional cycles of responses to stressful situational triggers. Workers can also facilitate the person to develop functional responses that become strengths that he/she can use to facilitate changes in the targeted area and other issues in his/her life.

In our SBCBT model, theoretically, the main thread of the intervention process is still very much a strength-based approach, helping an individual develop meaningful personal life goals, facilitating him/her to derive action plans, encouraging him/her to identify and use personal strengths and external resources to achieve the goals, and finding ways of overcoming the personal and environmental obstacles to goal attainment (Figure 1.1). From the very beginning, the worker has already adopted a strength perspective in working with the individual client.

Practice consideration

In the literature, there exist a number of well-developed strength-based approaches that have been adopted for practice for people with mental health concerns. These include Strengths-Based Interventions (SBI), Illness Management and Recovery Programme (IMR), and the Collaborative Recovery Model (CRM). While all of these approaches share similar characteristics of a recovery orientation: emphasizing a client's strengths and personal growth, facilitating goal setting and goal attainment, and so on, these approaches have been criticized for their (1) lack of standardized protocol, with some approaches focusing on self-directed strengths orientation, and others leaning towards a rehabilitative orientation; and (2) lack of a clear set of recovery-oriented intervention strategies, with some approaches having more specific strategies and others lacking (Tse et al, 2016).

From a practice point of view, many CBT techniques, which are structured and have well-developed procedures (e.g., worksheets and exercises), can be used or modified for use as strength-based intervention strategies. In our SBCBT approach, we use some of the conventional CBT techniques such as Situational Self-Analysis and Dysfunctional Cycle Diagram to help a person to identify and be aware of his/her dysfunctional patterns of cognitive, affective, and behavioural responses, and to find out functional response patterns that are effective in attaining identified goals and overcoming obstacles in the recovery process. Furthermore, in its original framework, CBT has already developed concrete and specific techniques for goal formulation and implementation; these tools and techniques can be readily adapted to the SBCBT model to help people with mental illness formulate concrete plans to achieve their goals.

In addition, CBT tools and techniques can be further modified to become strength-focused and be applied at different stages of our seven-stage SBCBT model. For example, at the stage of identifying and exploring resources, Life Review Exercise, which was originally used to understand a client's development of dysfunctional core beliefs, can be adapted to explore a client's internal and external resources, which can help him/her overcome life difficulties from the past. At the stage of developing tasks for achieving goals, behavioural experiments and exposure can be used to encourage the client to gain new positive and successful experiences in life. At the stage of continuous evaluation, a Piggy Bank technique can be applied to help a client record his/her positive experiences and be used as evidence to help the client build up a New Me.

Objectives of strength-based cognitive behaviour therapy

Our SBCBT bears the following objectives:

1 Helping clients build up hope and motivation in their recovery process, in order for them to achieve their life goals and give meaning to their lives.
2 Helping clients identify their personal goals through SBCBT techniques.

3   Helping clients explore and develop their personal interests, strengths, and aspirations through SBCBT techniques.
4   Helping clients utilize SBCBT techniques to identify and overcome barriers to goal attainment.

Seven phases of SBCBT for people in mental health recovery

Under our SBCBT model for people in mental health recovery, an individual will go through seven phases of the recovery process. At each phase, different SBCBT strategies and techniques can be deployed to help a person with mental illness. Table 1.1 provides an overview of the phases and the phase-relevant strategies and techniques. Specific techniques and their applications will be covered in each of the upcoming chapters.

Phase I

The focus of the first phase of the recovery model is to instil a sense of hope, build relationship with the individual, and to help the person understand his/her current life circumstances. The tools, techniques, and skills that can be used are explained in the following sections.

Skills in identifying and validating individual strengths

Throughout the recovery process, workers need to develop sensitivity in identifying, acknowledging, and validating the strengths and positive attributes of the person with mental illness. In the initial phase of the recovery process, this set of skills is extremely important as the skills can instil a sense of hope and enhance motivation for change in the person with mental illness. In addition, the validation can set the stage for creating a different perspective/atmosphere — focused on strengths rather than deficits — in the person with mental illness.

Normalization

The purpose of normalization is to educate the individual that everyone can develop varying degrees of mental health problems. One's experience with psychiatric symptoms is not totally unexplainable and alien to others. Indeed, the person's psychiatric experiences can often be related to his/her life experience in the past. In addition, the severity of the symptoms varies over time and the impacts to daily living therefore fluctuate (i.e., the symptoms would not affect the person with the same intensity all the time). In the recovery process, we have to educate the person with mental illness that his/her experience is not as 'weird' as some may think, and that the interpretation of such experience is often shaped by past life experiences. For instance, hearing

Table 1.1 The seven phases of SBCBT for people in mental health recovery

Phase of service	Techniques and tools
Phase I: Instilling hope and motivation to change	1 Relationship building 2 Motivational interviewing • Validation • Normalization • Be curious 3 Detecting dysfunctional responses in life situations • Situational Self-Analysis Exercise • Identify negative automatic thoughts • Emotion Thermometer
Phase II: Identifying needs	1 Helping the client to understand his/her circumstances • Dysfunctional and Functional Cycle Diagrams 2 Identifying interests and aspirations of the person with mental illness • Life Priorities Game
Phase III: Formulating and developing goals	1 Identifying short-term and long-term goals • Personal Strengths Assessment Form • Brainstorming • Pie Chart • Life Goal Formulation Chart 2 Evaluating the relative importance of the goals and their attainment feasibility
Phase IV: Exploring internal strengths and external resources	1 Identifying the internal and external resources of the person with mental illness • Personal Strengths Assessment Form • Life Review Exercise • Internal and External Resource Inventory
Phase V: Setting up tasks, strategies, and plans in achieving the goals	1 Prioritizing goals • Encouraging the person's participation in the setting up and execution of the strategies • The 5 Strategies 2 Behaviour approach to overcoming cognitive blind sport • Behaviour Experiment
Phase VI: Identifying individual or environmental barriers to achieving goals	1 Creating new experience to changing cognitive schemas and dysfunctional behavioural responses • Developing and staging the new experience 2 Identifying rigid dysfunctional values and rules in life • Costs and Benefits Analysis • Rewriting one's dysfunctional rules
Phase VII: Engaging in continuous review and feedback	1 Reviewing and consolidating lessons learned • Old Me/New Me Exercise • Piggy Bank Technique

voices (e.g., harsh criticisms towards self) during episodes of hallucination might reflect that a person is afraid of being criticized, and that such feelings might be related to his/her unhappy past experience of being criticized by significant others. Nonetheless, it is natural to dislike being criticized — a feeling that is common to all of us.

Furthermore, normalization skills can also help the person accept the limitations imposed by the illness, and not to push him/herself to change too quickly. Similarly, every one of us is bound to face many difficulties and challenges in life and has to walk through them one day at a time. While it is joyous to be able to successfully overcome the difficulties, it is equally important for the person to learn and accept that there are times when we feel temporarily stuck in certain situations. Normalization skills are particularly important under the recovery model. In the recovery process, it is very easy for the person to feel frustrated or lose morale when facing challenging situations. The normalization approach can increase the person's level of self-acceptance, and can help set more realistic expectations of oneself.

Curiosity

The worker should show a sense of curiosity rather than inadvertently create an impression of condemnation or criticisms towards the past and current experiences, personal needs, strengths, and resources of the person with mental illness. Such curiosity conveys a sense of interest in trying to understand the person, and demonstrates unconditional support, trust, and respect towards the person. This curiosity and interest ideally will help an individual feel valued and worthy. Incidentally, this can help to enhance his/her sense of hope and motivation to change.

Situational Self-Analysis and the Emotion Thermometer

CBT techniques commonly used in our SBCBT framework include Situational Self-Analysis and the Emotion Thermometer. Through sharing of the change in emotional state in the past week(s) (i.e., from 0 to 10, how will you rate your average mood state over the period) and of specific life events (i.e., event-based exploration), the workers help the individual explore and analyze his/her automatic physiological, cognitive, behavioural, and emotional response patterns to similar and varied situations. The core issue here is to identify possible dysfunctional cycles that keep the person in the trapped self (i.e., obstacles to goal attainment). When the person gains a clearer understanding of the response patterns, he/she will be encouraged to find ways of breaking the cycle. With increased positive experiences, it is hoped that the person's motivation to change will further increase and his/her hopes will be rekindled.

These techniques can also help the individual understand his/her interests. Take Linda as an example. She reported an improved mood state during the past week when she saw the worker. The average score of the Emotion Thermometer in the week was 6.5. Being curious, the worker asked Linda the reason for the increase from a score of 4 the week before to a score of 6.5 that week. Linda told the worker that she had had a gathering with her old schoolmates. In the gathering, they recalled happy memories (emotion) of working together on handicrafts and painting works and regained a sense of achievement (cognition), so much so that she had a strong urge to do it again (behaviour). Linda told the worker that she used to enjoy painting and paper cutting, and her works had been praised by the teacher. The worker grasped this opportunity to discuss with her if she would like to pick up this interest again, encouraging her to set up a timetable to carry it out.

Phase II

The task of Phase II is to help the individual understand his/her needs while paving the way for the next phase of goal setting in the recovery process. The following tools and techniques can be used in this phase.

Understanding one's functional and dysfunctional cycle

When facing life events, people habitually respond with certain patterned thoughts, emotions, and behaviours. When these responses are dysfunctional, they may generate negative emotions, thoughts, and behaviours. Such responses could be met with disapproval from others, creating a negative spiral of responses from the person again. Consequently, this results in a vicious cycle. Again, take the case of Linda to illustrate the point. Linda habitually felt suspicious of people's motives. She was then in her twenties and had suffered from schizophrenia since she was in grade 12. Oftentimes, Linda thought that people were laughing at her and that her schoolmates found her lazy and ugly. When the symptoms became severe, she got very panicky, avoided seeing people, and did not go to school. Eventually, she was sent by the family to consult a psychiatrist. Since then, her condition had improved and stabilized under medications. Linda moved on to college and in the first few weeks of school, she told the worker that her teacher gave her a critical look, and that he judged her to be lazy and inattentive. When she had those thoughts, she felt unhappy and panicky; at the same time, she felt her heartbeat racing. When this happened, Linda had the thought of leaving the classroom immediately. The more she avoided this kind of situation, the more panicky and self-defeating she became. Gradually, she withdrew more and more to herself and become more paranoid of others. This had been Linda's habitual dysfunctional cycle of responses.

However, in this scenario, Linda did not leave the classroom. She reminded herself to try to stay in that environment and focused on her study. Although she found it very difficult to concentrate, she had not escaped and she felt a sense of satisfaction when the class was over. The worker reviewed the situation with her and helped her draw the functional cycle of responses. She was able to see that if she changed her habitual cognitive and behavioural responses (i.e., avoidance and 'I can't deal with this'), she was able to reduce her sense of panic and could stop her avoidance behaviour. Linda was then asked to continue to practice these new cognitive and behavioural responses.

The Life Priorities Game

The Life Priorities Game helps the person examine his/her priorities concerning various life goals and aspirations. The worksheet comprises 12 blank cells, representing a variety of life domains, including family, friends, work, personal interest, and so on. The worker tells the person that he/she is given one million dollars (i.e., representing the time he/she has) and that he/she has to allocate the money to various cells, with a higher amount implying more time being spent or would like to spend in the area. Beside each dimension are two columns, one stating the current life situation and another column representing the ideal situation. The person has to put money into the life domains he/she chooses, with each column having a total of one million dollars. When this is finished, differences in the allocation of monies would be highlighted by the worker to help the individual reflect on what he/she wants in his/her life. For example, suppose the person indicates that he/she has allocated 0.6 million in 'playing computer games at home' (that is spending 60% of time in playing computer games), but in an ideal world, he/she would want to allocate only 0.3 million to this cell and put the remaining 0.3 million in making friends or going to work. The worker would highlight the differences in the allocations and review with him/her what he/she really wants for him/herself. This exercise can help the individual to understand his/her needs, and to develop motivations and plans to achieve the goals.

Phase III

The focus of Phase III is to help the person set goals based on his/her needs or aspirations. There are short-term and long-term goals. Well-set short-term and long-term goals lead the individual to formulate concrete strategies and action plans. The following are some of the techniques.

Personal Strengths Assessment form

With the use of a detailed Strengths Assessment form, the individual has to answer various questions about his/her life circumstances, aspirations, and resources in relation to living environment, transportation, finance, work/education, social life, health, leisure activities, and so on. The person is asked to think these through and decide on the top three areas in which he/she wishes to achieve. In addition to use in Phase III, this form is also relevant to Phase II concerning identifying needs and Phase IV in exploring internal and external resources. This tool will be discussed in detail in Chapter 3.

Brainstorming

A simple technique to set goals is brainstorming. The individual is asked to write on a piece of paper what he/she likes or wants in life, and explain the reason(s) why he/she says so. The worker can help the person consolidate and prioritize these goals.

Phase IV

The task in Phase IV is to explore with the person his/her internal and external strengths and resources, as well as how he/she can use the resources to achieve the goals.

Life Review Exercise

Using the Life Review worksheet, the worker can invite the individual to share significant happy life experiences and events that hold special meaning for him/her in the past and currently. All experiences in his/her childhood, adolescence, and/or adulthood can be explored. In each event, the worker examines carefully what has given the individual a sense of satisfaction and happiness, taking note of the particular external and internal resources that have been instrumental in leading to such happiness and satisfaction. Even though some of the external/internal resources may no longer be available, the worker can explore with the person ways to re-develop those resources. At the same time, the worker can also help the person explore and develop new and potential resources.

Internal and external resource inventory

Another simple and useful technique is to invite the person to make a resource inventory. The client can list out his/her internal and external resources, and then examine which of those resources he/she may find helpful in achieving the goals. This technique can be used with people who have better cognitive abilities and better personal insights.

Phase V

The purpose of Phase V is to work with the person in setting feasible tasks, strategies, and plans to achieve the set goals.

Encouraging participation in formulating and executing the strategies

The recovery model is basically client-led and the person is expected to be highly autonomous in setting the goals, strategies, and plans. It is important to encourage the individual to participate in working out a feasible and effective action plan to enhance his/her motivation to take action. During the process, the worker has to patiently and continuously encourage the person to taking the first step; as the first can often be the most difficult to take. After all, the person might have been rather complacent in his/her comfort zone or might have negative past experiences that psychologically hinder him/her from taking the step forward. However, once the client has a taste of initial success, the worker can then continue to encourage him/her to take the second and third steps. During this period of implementation, the worker needs to help the person examine and revise the strategies or action plan, if needed. The principle is: Continue to do what works and drop what doesn't work.

The 5-Strategies

The 5-Strategies have been developed to help an individual break the dysfunctional cycle of responses. During the recovery process, one area in which the 5-Strategies can be effectively used is to manage negative emotions of an individual. When these negative emotions are not well handled, they may affect the person's progress in achieving his/her goals. The 5-Strategies include: (1) raising awareness of the physiological alarm signals, (2) stopping the negative thoughts, (3) using self-questioning techniques, (4) engaging in distractions to prevent indulging in negative thoughts, and (5) developing positive self-statements.

Take the case of Linda as an example again. Linda could easily have automatic self-defeating thoughts that would lead her to give up the plans in achieving her goals. In her recovery process, at one time, she registered for a drawing class and felt that the staff was rather indifferent to her. She sensed her frustration (emotional response) and felt a stone pressing heavily on her chest (physiological response). Linda believed that the staff was commenting on her inability to draw properly. She then repeatedly told herself that it was a waste of time and her efforts would be futile (cognitive responses: self-defeating, making rash conclusions based on inadequate evidence). In the end, Linda decided to leave without registering for the course (behavioural response). The worker helped Linda use the 5-Strategies to overcome her difficulties. Linda realized that she needed to stop the negative thoughts, and she chose to use deep breathing (i.e., stopping the negative thoughts) and shifted her focus by looking at a piece of handicraft that made her proud because it was praised by a teacher when she was in high school (i.e., distraction). At the same time, she would remind herself that 'if I don't try, I couldn't do anything. Do I really want that?' (self-questioning).

The positive self-statement she developed later was, 'As long as you have tried, the outcome is unimportant'. When the 5-Strategies were developed, Linda was asked to practice the strategies and she later felt more calm and in control of her negative emotions.

Phase VI

There are bound to be difficulties and barriers in the road to achieving the goals. Barriers can come from the individual or from the environment. The major task in Phase VI is to work with the person to identify those barriers and explore ways to overcome them. The following tools can be used.

Creating New Experiences

Barriers to goal attainment may originate from deep-rooted beliefs. For example, a person may have the belief that he/she can never be able to change the situation, and hence, give up taking the first step in achieving the goals. One way of changing these dysfunctional beliefs is to create new and positive experiences for the person. This technique mainly involves creating opportunities for the person to try something new and different. With every new experience, the old perspective can be challenged and new beliefs can be gradually formed.

Costs and Benefits Analysis

Another way of overcoming dysfunctional beliefs associated with barriers to goal attainment is to engage the person in a Costs and Benefits Analysis of holding onto a belief. The worker can explore further how these rules can be rewritten to become more functional.

The above two techniques will be described in more detail in Chapters 7 and 8.

Phase VII

In different phases of recovery, the person faces many different challenging situations that make him/her unable to smoothly achieve his/her goals. The worker should conduct regular reviews on the progress and provide feedback and encouragement for the person. Through these reviews, the person can increase his/her self-understanding, learn to own the process of change, and provide self-reinforcement. In addition, the worker should acknowledge and appreciate the efforts, abilities, and achievements of the person to instil a sense of confidence in the person. It is hoped that, in the long run, the person can continue with the road to recovery independently. Two techniques can be used.

Old Me/New Me

The Old Me/New Me technique helps the individual reflect on the differences between how he/she was before and how he/she is now. For example, the Old Me could be more passive, tended to back down when facing difficulties, and dared not to try new things. On the other hand, the New Me has a new sense of self, and is able to acknowledge his/her own strengths gained in the process of recovery. Writing down descriptions of the Old Me and New Me and providing concrete evidence of the changes allows the person to further validate his/her own values.

Piggy Bank technique

Another similar strategy is to invite the person to write down what he/she has done successfully and put each successful experience in a piggy bank. Through the collection of positive experiences, it is hoped that the person can really see his/her gains and become even more motivated. It is common for people to remember failures and forget successes. The Piggy Bank technique can literally 'save up' the success stories so that the experiences can be remembered. Indeed, these reminders can serve as evidence when doing the Old Me/New Me exercise.

Critiques of strength–based recovery models

Although the concept of strength-based recovery is now widely adopted and practiced in the mental health field, some criticize that this concept can become too dogmatic if every staff member is expected to follow the model. Moreover, if any deviation from the recovery perspective is criticized as deviating from the normal and the 'best' practice, there will be very little room to explore alternative and perhaps equally effective approaches.

Is the strength-based recovery concept an all-encompassing concept applicable in all situations? As mentioned in the previous section, practical considerations such as social and environmental resources and constraints, and cultural backgrounds that facilitate or impede the acceptance of the strength-based recovery concept, should be considered for the successful implementation of the recovery model (Jones-Smith, 2012). Time is needed to change certain social and environmental constraints in some countries and regions before a full implementation of the recovery model can become feasible.

In addition, the effectiveness of the strength-based recovery approach also depends on the abilities and conditions of the individual. Some people with mental illness do not see the need to set life goals, let alone take steps to achieve those goals. For some, this is not what they want to do.

Lastly, this approach may bring false hope for some people. Some people may not have the capacity to achieve the goals they want to set for themselves.

They may feel frustrated if they cannot achieve their goals. People around the person with mental illness may also feel defeated or criticized and may blame the person for not trying hard enough.

Conclusion

This chapter introduced the concepts and principles of recovery and argues that the CBT approach and recovery concepts can be meaningfully integrated to provide a sound theoretical and practical approach in working with people with mental health problems. The later part of the chapter provided an overview of the seven phases of the SBCBT model for people in mental health recovery and illustrated with case examples how the different phases unfold during the recovery process. Lastly, although the recovery concepts have been widely accepted and practiced in many countries and regions, there are criticisms of the concepts that are worth pondering when applying to a specific sociocultural context.

2 Two stories on strength–based cognitive behaviour therapy in mental health recovery

Introduction

In the previous chapter, we explained the differences between rehabilitation and recovery and described the seven phases of the strength-based cognitive behaviour therapy (SBCBT) model in the mental health recovery process. In this chapter, we will illustrate how SBCBT is applied in each phase using two case illustrations. We will demonstrate how SBCBT strategies can be applied flexibly in the different phases — from motivating the client to change, formulating personal goals, taking actions, and achieving the goals.

The recovery process of Jenny

Background

Jenny's mother was an anxiety-prone person; as a child, Jenny was brought up in a very strict and restrained environment. Worrying about the safety of Jenny, her mother forbade her to stay out late, let alone sleeping over at friends' houses. Unlike her young peers, Jenny was not allowed to join social activities and go to camps. Due to the restrictions in her social life and her mother's overprotectiveness, Jenny's social and peer relationships were adversely affected, and she lacked opportunities to develop her social skills and problem-solving abilities. Like her mother, Jenny also tended to get anxious very easily.

At the age of 26, Jenny started to develop symptoms of schizophrenia due to stress at work. She felt that she was being followed and everyone was trying to harm her. She lost trust in the people around her and felt that the world was a dangerous place in which to live. Her anxiety level increased and she often was low in mood, had insomnia, and experienced poor sleep quality. Jenny's family members then took her to the hospital for treatment. After medical treatment, most of the symptoms were under control. However, the medication could help her to only some extent; in day-to-day life, she was still a worrier and was highly anxious.

Three months after Jenny was discharged from the hospital, she was referred to the Integrated Community Centre for Mental Wellness (i.e., a type of community-based mental health day centre in Hong Kong) for the purpose of encouraging her to participate in more social activities. Jenny joined the day programmes of the centre and started counselling service for her recovery.

Intervention process

Phase I: Instilling hope and motivation to change

Jenny was considered a very compliant person. She was still looking for a job when she was referred to the centre and was willing to join the centre's activities to kill time. However, Jenny had no concrete idea regarding her own recovery.

Jenny had some insight into her problem. She realized that her anxiety had somehow affected her ability to keep a job. Based on past experience, it was not difficult for Jenny to get a job interview and an offer. The issue was her tendency to give up easily when she encountered difficulties. The experience of her illness had an enormous impact on her and any stressful situation would trigger her automatic thoughts such as: 'I definitely couldn't do it!' and 'I'm going to have a relapse!' She became extremely anxious and eventually chose to escape. Jenny would associate common interview questions with potential work stress she might face in the future, and then visualized herself having a relapse due to stress. Because Jenny's onset of illness was triggered by work stress, she was very concerned about returning to work again. The worker felt that Jenny was moderately motivated to change; however, she did not know how to overcome her anxiety. As a result, she was uncertain about the future and dare not hold out any hope. The first step in the recovery process was to help Jenny find hopes and motivations to get out of her state of inertia.

Initially, Jenny did not know why she was more prone to anxiety in comparison with others, and she felt that she had no way out. Through the Situational Self-Analysis exercise, Jenny became aware of her emotional, physical, cognitive, and behavioural response patterns; their interrelatedness; and the vicious cycle that was formed among these responses.

Using the cognitive behaviour therapy (CBT) technique of drawing a Dysfunctional Cycle Diagram, the worker helped Jenny realize that whenever she encountered any difficulty, she would automatically come up with certain catastrophizing thoughts, whereby she would amplify the seriousness of the problem and underestimate her ability to cope with the difficulty. Together with Jenny's tendency to feel overly anxious about having a relapse, she opted to take the 'safest' step — escape from the situation. In doing so, Jenny had created many experiences of failure for herself, reinforcing her belief that she was not capable of solving life's problems. Subsequently, her fear of facing difficulties increased even further. The diagram of the

Dysfunction Cycle not only highlighted Jenny's response patterns and the core issues she was facing, but it also increased her insight and motivation for change as she could now see ways out of her inertia. She saw her difficulty from a new perspective and understood that it was important for her to deal with her anxiety and make changes.

Phase II: Identifying needs

On further exploration, the worker found that apart from challenges at work, Jenny's anxiety also came from interpersonal relationship issues because she felt scared and nervous in front of others, particularly strangers. She always had a feeling that her colleagues were talking behind her back, and as a consequence, she would withdraw from social interactions. Unfortunately, the more she did this, the more anxious she became as she thought that was the only way out of her anxiety. The fear of social contact thus constituted another major obstacle in her recovery. Ironically, as we observed, her abilities were not as poor as she had imagined.

The worker reassured Jenny that it was normal to feel nervous when facing new challenges, and physical signs such as increased heartbeat, sweating, lack of appetite, and muscle tension were generally normal bodily responses. Because of anxieties, Jenny used to turn blank-eyed and spaced-out as if her body were a machine that had temporarily stopped running. She would stop what she was doing, imagining those responses as signs of a relapse, and become even more nervous. By 'normalizing' some of her physiological responses, Jenny became less overwhelmed by her own anxiety and she was helped to stop escalating her negative emotions.

In the early stage of the recovery process, Jenny filled out the Personal Strengths Assessment form. One thing we noticed was that Jenny shared similar aspirations as her peers. She wished to be gainfully employed and be able to make plans for the future. To achieve these aspirations, Jenny understood that what she needed most was to break the vicious cycles.

Phase III: Formulating and developing goals

Initially, finding a job was Jenny's goal in recovery. After exploration, she understood that she had to overcome her anxiety in order to keep a job. Jenny was helped to understand that she needed to modify her physiological, cognitive, emotional, and behavioural response patterns. In addition, apart from managing her anxieties, Jenny needed to deal with her sense of incompetence, which also contributed to her anxiety problems. Thus, another goal in recovery was to find ways of enhancing her sense of competence. The worker then made plans to meet Jenny on a biweekly basis.

As said, Jenny had no problem in getting a job, which she did earlier on in our engagement. With the new insights she had gained, together with the support and guidance of the worker, Jenny was able to overcome her anxiety gradually. Whereas she would have quitted her job easily before, she now set a short-term goal to keep the job at least for the three-month probationary period.

Phase IV: Exploring internal strengths and external resources

Although Jenny had many strengths and resources, she was not aware of them due to her lack of confidence. When people praised her strengths, she would just deny her abilities. In this regard, the Personal Strengths Assessment form is an excellent tool to assist the client in exploring these resources. This form helped Jenny to identify her previously unaware strengths and resources. Completing the form showed that Jenny had good interpersonal relationships with some close friends and family members. At the same time, she was also receiving counselling and was actively participating in centre activities — which contributed to her pool of community resources. All in all, Jenny started to recognize that she had a very good support network that could provide tremendous help in her road to recovery.

Although Jenny had had some positive experiences in life, she used to ignore or play down those experiences. The worker used a Pie Chart to help her recall past successful interview experiences, and analyzed the extent to which the successes were attributed to her personal abilities or external factors. Initially, Jenny attributed those positive experiences to external factors such as the kindness of the boss, support from family members, luck, and so on. She adamantly believed that her successes were due to the efforts of others and she had played no part in the successes. After careful analysis, Jenny started to recognize how her own personal strengths had contributed to those positive experiences. For example, she realized that she was also willing to try and that her performance was good during interviews. The worker pointed out that her willingness to take risks was an important factor in her recovery, and Jenny started to feel more confident in herself. Rather than belittling herself, Jenny started to learn to appreciate herself.

The worker identified some positive personality traits of Jenny by observing her performance in the centre activities. It was noticed that Jenny was always punctual, was able to keep her word, fulfilled her tasks seriously and carefully, and she was responsible, committed, and willing to work as a team. Embracing the strength-based approach, the worker communicated directly to Jenny these positive traits and internal resources. The praise and recognition by the worker validated Jenny's ability for self-appreciation and she became more capable of identifying her own strengths.

Phase V: Setting up tasks, strategies, and plans in achieving the goals

Gradually, Jenny made progress in achieving her goals in recovery. In terms of enhancing Jenny's feeling of competence, the worker suggested that Jenny could build her good work attitude — she took her job seriously and responsibly. Jenny started to work as an activity assistant in the centre, helping out in various small tasks such as doing centre decoration and leading simple games/activities for group members. Jenny was happy to try, despite making some minor mistakes initially. With encouragement, Jenny was willing to deal with challenges in the process. Her personal strengths enabled her to perform better and better in her post and she was able to accumulate further successful experiences.

As Jenny became more confident in herself, the worker started to work on her social and work anxieties. To begin with, the worker asked Jenny to list and prioritize all possible scenarios that might make her feel anxious. Starting from the least anxiety-inducing scenarios, the exposure technique was used to help her overcome the negative emotions. For Jenny, the scenario that made her most anxious was 'meeting strangers', followed by 'sustaining a conversation with a fellow member', 'standing in front of a crowd', 'leading warm-up exercise', and 'sharing experiences in recovery'. To tackle the different situations, the worker designed relevant tasks for Jenny. Using the 5-Strategies (5S) technique, she was helped to develop practical strategies to manage her anxiety. In most situations, Jenny needed the presence of someone she trusted to boost her confidence. At times, the worker would encourage her to tackle the situation independently and Jenny was able to make progress gradually.

To tackle Jenny's fear of job interviews, the worker used role play to explore possible questions that might come up in the interview. Through these practices, Jenny was helped to understand how she was affected by her negative automatic thoughts. She was able to identify her thought trap of 'catastrophizing', become aware of her anxiety quickly, and learned to use 5S to stop the negative thoughts. Understanding her own thinking pattern was a critical step for Jenny to overcome her feeling of anxiety.

After finishing the exercise on exposure, the next step Jenny decided to take was to start a practicum as a clerk in a company through the arrangement of the centre. In terms of possible barriers and developing strategies to manage them, after discussing with the worker, Jenny decided that if and when the thought of quitting the job appeared in her mind, she would meet face-to-face with the worker first before making any final decision. During the probationary period in working as a clerk, the vicious cycle that the worker had discussed with Jenny appeared repeatedly. However, Jenny was able to hold on to her thoughts and feelings without actually submitting her resignation. This demonstrated to Jenny that she had the capacity to cope with anxiety without quitting. Ironically, in line with Jenny's thinking pattern, Jenny did not see this success as a result of her own effort. The worker had to facilitate her to reflect on her effort in making this possible, and eventually, Jenny was able to realize that her perseverance could be a strength she could further develop. This increased Jenny's overall sense of competence.

As Jenny was beginning to feel more confident, the worker used the Functional Cycle Diagram to examine the positive factors contributing to her successful changes. Similar to the Dysfunction Cycle Diagram that identified dysfunctional patterns; the Functional Cycle Diagram served to identify factors and patterns leading to positive changes in a client and helped the person sustain his/her motivation for change.

Phase VI: Identifying individual or environmental barriers to achieving goals

It is natural for people to put up a defence or get away from anxiety-provoking situations. In the case of Jenny, whenever she developed catastrophic thoughts, her immediate response was to get away by quitting the job. In the exposure exercise and during the practicum, Jenny often thought of giving up and wanted to escape from the situation. With increasing positive experiences, Jenny was able to overcome this obstacle.

Jenny also encountered some other barriers in trying to achieve her goals. During the practicum, Jenny became very anxious because she did not know how to construct an e-form for data entry. She was overwhelmed by the fear of failure and relapse and considered quitting the job. Understanding what was going on, Jenny used the 5S technique to tackle her negative emotions. She took a deep breath and tried to clear her mind by staying in the washroom for a while. This helped her to stop dwelling on her negative thoughts. Later, when she was helped to reflect on the incident, Jenny realized that it was not as bad as she had thought and that she was capable of handling the situation. In this phase, Jenny was more able to take charge of the situation on her own. Through biweekly meetings, the worker gave Jenny feedback and affirmed her abilities in dealing with her difficulties.

Jenny had a constant fear of relapse, though she did not have much knowledge about it. Having no sense of control is common for people suffering from mental illness. In Jenny's mindset, relapse was inevitable and there was nothing she could do. Her worry was so real to her that if she were to lose her appetite for just a single day, she felt it was a sure sign of relapse. The worker educated Jenny about schizophrenia, its signs and symptoms of relapse, relapse prevention, and mental illness management.

Phase VII: Engaging in continuous review and feedback

Eventually, Jenny was able to achieve the goal of finishing the three-month probationary period at her job. Throughout the period, the worker touched base continuously with Jenny to help her overcome her barriers. She was helped to explore factors contributing to her successful experiences and was able to replace the previous dysfunctional cycle with a functional cycle. Her confidence began to grow after realizing her strengths and abilities.

The worker also used the Old Me/New Me technique to compare Jenny's differences from when she first started the service. After the review, Jenny was further reassured of the role she had actively played in making the positive changes she had achieved. This further increased her feeling of competence.

With the achievement of the set goals and at the end of the practicum period for Jenny, and with the achievement Jenny had maintained, the case was closed. Jenny no longer needed to rely on the worker and was ready to start a new chapter in life.

Outcome

The recovery process opened up a very different life story for Jenny. Her fear of relapse was significantly reduced and she no longer gave up easily. Jenny was more aware of her in-depth feelings and became more sensitive to the impact of her anxiety. She recognized her own abilities and strengths, was more confident that she could manage her work, and her sense of competence increased. With this new-found confidence, Jenny became more independent.

The company where Jenny did her practicum was satisfied with her performance and extended her contract. The job not only provided an opportunity for Jenny to utilize her potential, it also increased her sense of self-worth. Jenny's active participation in the process had helped her find an identity and a role in the community. At work, Jenny felt more confident in communicating with her colleagues and she became more at ease in interpersonal relationships.

The recovery process of Ann

Most service recipients at the mental health service centre may not be totally ready to engage in the recovery process. The worker has to keep pace with them and try to motivate them to start the journey to recovery.

Background

Ann was a 39-year-old single woman. She had two younger brothers and her parents divorced when she was in grade 10. Later, her mother remarried and moved out to live with her second husband. Ann used to live with her younger brother, but their relationship was very poor and conflicts occurred frequently.

Ann was an introvert; she did not trust people easily and did not like to share her private life with others. Because Ann did not want to live with her brothers, she moved frequently and had once stayed with her boyfriend. Eventually, Ann was admitted into a halfway house. As she usually did not stay in a place for long, it was difficult for her to develop a sense of security with people around her and with the environment.

Ann was diagnosed with depression in 2009. When she was having depressive episodes, she would have many negative automatic thoughts and suicidal ideations. Family conflicts further worsened her depression. Ann started recovery service in 2014 when she was staying in a halfway house.

Initially, she resisted any help, as she just wanted a place to stay. She told the worker that she came to the halfway house simply because she had no choice and she interacted with the worker with much reluctance.

Intervention

Phase I: Instilling hope and motivation to change

The first task of the worker was to build up a trusting relationship with Ann. When Ann first came to the halfway house, she tended to lose her temper easily and had frequent conflicts with her housemates. Instead of enforcing house rules, the worker showed empathy and acceptance and tried to lower her resistance.

Furthermore, to reduce Ann's defence, the worker tried to create a more relaxed atmosphere by replacing formal counselling with informal daily encounters. In addition, the worker praised her efforts in agreeing to receive services offered by the halfway house and reassured her that this was the first step to change.

Because Ann had frequent conflicts with her family members, she felt that she had no other option but to stay in the halfway house and complied with the house rules. In fact, having 'no choice' in life was a common feeling expressed by Ann. The worker acknowledged her feelings and reassured her that it was completely her choice and decision in setting her own goals and plans for recovery.

This had effectively instilled a sense of hope and motivation in Ann, and reassured her that she could take charge of her own life. Ann started to assess her situation from a different perspective and realized that she could make use of the resources provided by the halfway house to make plans and to help her in recovery. She started to gain more insight and saw her condition in a more positive light.

Phase II: Identifying needs

The worker went through the Personal Strengths Assessment form with Ann to explore the resources, strengths, and aspirations she possessed. The form was very effective in identifying the unexplored artistic talent of Ann. In the process, she was also helped to identify her weaknesses.

When the worker was going through the form with Ann, it was noted that between her first onset in 2009 and her admission to the halfway house in 2014, Ann had not been gainfully employed. Therefore, she was unaware of the current conditions in the labour market. For example, her understanding of the courses offered by the Employees Retraining Board (ERB — a Hong Kong government agency that provides job retraining for people who are unemployed or underemployed) still very much related to traditional courses such as training to become home helpers and security guards. These courses were considered to be dated. Ann did not realize that current course offerings were much more diversified, such as flower arrangement, barista training, and so on. The worker had to introduce current information to her to supplement her inadequate knowledge.

In this phase, the worker noted that Ann was not yet ready to deal with her personal issues. In addition, it was also noticed that Ann had only limited knowledge about depression. She relied too much on her own feelings and did not trust the psychiatrist. She just stopped taking medications when she 'felt' herself having a better mood. Furthermore, she argued with the psychiatrists on the types and dosages of medications to be taken without justification. She did not seem to understand and manage her own emotions well. She thought she was already doing quite well emotionally, but, in fact, she tended to lose her temper easily with just a slight trigger. Obviously, emotional management was an issue for Ann but she did not seem to be aware of it yet. The worker tried to keep pace with her and let her deal with issues she considered more important first.

Phase III: Formulating and developing goals

Ann had many unsuccessful experiences in the job market such as failing job interviews, feeling inadequate to perform, and quitting a job in one to two days. Many times, these job issues were caused by poor interpersonal relationships. These negative experiences became a barrier for Ann in seeking jobs and she would just faint-heartedly browse the recruitment advertisements without actually doing anything to apply for a job. Indeed, she was afraid of failing again and was socially anxious.

In the section on personal goals under the Personal Strengths Assessment form, Ann wrote down three goals: (1) find a job; (2) make improvements in interpersonal relationship; and (3) live independently. It was common for recovering persons to consider getting a job as a critical step in solving all their problems. Similarly, Ann thought that as long as she had a job, it could offer her mental support and naturally, her mental condition and everything else would improve and she could live independently. But Ann was unemployed for a considerable period of time. She was trapped in the vicious cycle of considering herself a failure; she was frustrated and became even more disturbed emotionally. On the other hand, her dysfunctional emotional management approach also created another vicious cycle of poor interpersonal relationship. At this stage, the primary focus of the worker was to help her sort out her priorities.

The worker used a common CBT technique of drawing a Dysfunctional Cycle Diagram to help Ann realize the mechanisms of her vicious cycle. To use Ann's interpersonal relationship in the halfway house as an illustration, Ann was very impatient with both the staff and the housemates, which often ended up in her having temper outbursts and storming out of the room. In any conflictual interpersonal relationship, Ann would begin suppressing her emotions and did not air her feelings properly. When she could not hold her temper any longer, she would have an angry outburst. However, when she displayed these outbursts, she became even more upset afterwards, as she worried that people might judge her negatively. Eventually, this became a repeated pattern of responses in Ann's conflictual interpersonal relationships.

After building up a trusting relationship, the worker helped Ann to understand the impact of her emotional outbursts on others and how she could use a better way to express herself. Gradually, Ann realized that she should learn how to manage her emotions before she took steps to find a job. The ability to manage her emotions could improve her interpersonal relationship, increase her chance to keep stable employment, and allow her to be financially independent.

Another CBT strategy the worker had used with Ann was the Situational Self-Analysis exercise to examine her interaction pattern with halfway-house staff. Through analyzing real-life situations, Ann was able to identify her thought trap of 'mind reading', thinking that the staff did not like her. After counter-checking her thoughts with the staff, she realized that it was not the case but she had acquired this kind of automatic response for many years. Indeed, this thought pattern had repeatedly and unconsciously been affecting her emotions negatively.

Ann eventually revised the priorities of her goals as follows:

1 to learn emotion management, attitudes, and skills in interpersonal relationships
2 to re-enter the job market and get a stable income, and
3 to live independently in her own space

Phase IV: Exploring internal strengths and external resources

Through the Personal Strengths Assessment form, Ann was able to identify her many internal strengths, as well as obtain information on available community resources and guidelines on how to utilize these resources in her recovery process.

In terms of her internal resources, Ann recalled her interests in painting and flower arrangement and that she was an artistic person. The worker then invited her to join the art group in the halfway house. Ann enjoyed the activities and was pleased with the compliments she received in the group. This new experience allowed her to use the talents she always possessed but might have forgotten since she had become ill.

With time, situations in which Ann formerly experienced barriers have turned out to be positive external resources. Ann preferred a quiet environment and did not like to trouble others. Therefore, what bothered her most while living in a hostel was the group living environment and the lack of personal space. After joining the art group, she received a lot of positive feedback from other group members. Then, Ann began to realize that many of her housemates had similar experiences as hers and it was easier to communicate and share their feelings. These friendships had become Ann's external resources. The worker also introduced to Ann art-related courses offered by the ERB. Through these external resources, Ann was able to develop her interests and potential.

Phase V: Setting up tasks, strategies, and plans in achieving the goals

At this stage, the worker had already built up a trusting relationship with Ann. Her motivation to change had increased tremendously and she would make active attempts to improve. The worker used other CBT strategies to help her manage her emotion further and move towards achieving her goals. The CBT strategies used included Emotion Thermometer, Situational Self-Analysis exercise, the 5-Strategies, and Creating New Experiences.

To illustrate, the automatic negative thought of Ann was that people did not like her (i.e., mind reading). Using the 5-Strategies, Ann started to use the self-questioning technique to explore if there was any evidence to support her impression of being disliked. Through this technique, Ann was able to avoid falling into her thought trap and the consequential unnecessary emotional disturbance.

The worker also helped Ann to write down her successful experiences in solving life difficulties, analyze the process, and then draw a Functional Cycle Diagram similar to that of the Dysfunctional Cycle Diagram.

To provide Ann with opportunities to use her strengths, the worker invited Ann to decorate the hostel during festivals. Ann was responsible for designing and decorating the house and she did a good job. This proved to be an effective way for Ann to demonstrate her talents and helped her build up confidence and her sense of competence.

Phase VI: Identifying individual or environmental barriers to achieving goals

With an increased level of self-understanding, Ann's changes were very obvious in this phase. One of the barriers for Ann in emotional management was her lack of trust in others due to her previous negative experiences in life. However, while staying in the halfway house, Ann started to do something differently and expressed her goodwill to a housemate with whom she had previous conflicts by giving the housemate a small gift. The response of the housemate was very positive. The worker made use of this real-life experience to help Ann understand that things might not be as rigid as she thought. When Ann was certain that people disliked her, she believed that a broken relationship would forever ensue. However, with this and other new experiences, Ann was helped to realize that it was possible to mend a tense relationship. This broadened her perspective and increased her willingness to consider alternatives.

Phase VII: Engaging in continuous review and feedback

CBT strategies and tools were used throughout the recovery process for Ann. For example, the Emotion Thermometer was used in every session to help Ann assess the change in her emotions; the Situational Self-Analysis exercise was used frequently to help her examine what she had experienced and to identify patterns of response. Furthermore, the worker also provided regular feedback to Ann so that she could be aware of the changes she had made and be alert to possible re-emergence of any old pattern.

Outcome

Through the seven phases in the SBCBT, Ann made significant improvements in her emotion management. The frequency of her temper outbursts had significantly decreased and Ann became more ready to share her feelings constructively. To a large extent, Ann was able to achieve the three goals she set for herself.

1 Her interpersonal relationship had improved because she had better emotion management.
2 She was able to find a stable job and stayed in the job for 6 months.
3 With the help of the worker, she applied for public housing and had lived independently since then.

Conclusion

This chapter has highlighted how SBCBT can play out in the mental health recovery process. The stories of Jenny and Ann show how SBCBT strategies can be sensibly and smoothly merged with a strength-based recovery process. In the following chapters, the phase-specific SBCBT strategies will be delineated, providing readers with detailed rationales, procedures, and case illustrations of how SBCBT strategies can be used to help people recover from mental illness.

3 Phase I: Instilling hope and motivation to change

Introduction

In the first phase of the recovery process, the focus is on instilling hope in clients and motivating them to change. This is a critical phase, as many clients are still in their trapped selves at the beginning of the recovery process. These clients are passive, have lost hope, and cannot envision any prospect for change. If the worker is able to raise clients' awareness of the nature of the trapped self, and help them understand factors contributing to the condition of trapped self, it would be a major discovery for these clients. Once clients understand why they are trapped, they may realize that they can transform their lives by making changes.

In the previous chapter, we provided an overview of two cases that illustrate how strength-based cognitive behaviour therapy (SBCBT) can be meaningfully applied in the recovery process. We also introduced a number of strategies that can be used in the initial phase to instil a sense of hope and motivation among clients in the recovery process. These strategies include: (1) appreciate and validate the strengths of the client, (2) help the client identify his/her dysfunctional or functional cycles in daily life, and (3) demonstrate a sense of curiosity towards clients' concerns. In this chapter, two sets of strategies and tools, namely, the Personal Strengths Assessment form and Situational Self-Analysis exercise and the Emotion Thermometer, will be described in detail to illustrate how these strategies can increase hope and motivation in clients in the recovery process.

Intervention tool: Personal Strengths Assessment form

In the initial stage of the SBCBT mental health recovery process, it is of interest to the worker to gain a thorough understanding of the needs, aspirations, and potential goals of a client. This also gives the client a clear message that the recovery process is client-directed and the role of the worker is to facilitate him/her to go through the process in a step-by-step fashion. The Personal Strengths Assessment form is an important tool to help the client in understanding his/her concerns, needs, and aspirations. The exercise aims to heighten the client's awareness of the above issues, but it also has the effect of instilling hope and motivation for the client to engage in something different from what he/she is currently doing (i.e., trapped self) and to potentially make a difference in his/her life (i.e., liberated self).

Case background

Mandy was in her fifties when she began meeting with the worker. She was diagnosed with depression in 2009. At that time, she had constant conflicts, even physical fights, with her husband due to communication and financial problems. Mandy's husband had very little knowledge about her illness. Their marriage relationship deteriorated, and the couple eventually divorced in 2011.

After Mandy divorced her husband, she wanted to return to her maiden home. However, her father refused to take her in for fear of being discriminated against in his social circle, because divorce was considered a disgrace to the family. Reluctantly, Mandy had to rent a subdivided unit (i.e., a cubicle) by herself. However, Mandy was unable to get a job with adequate pay to support herself financially. Therefore, she had no choice but to rent cheap, rundown accommodations. For several years after the divorce, Mandy could not find a permanent residence. Furthermore, she had been a full-time housewife after marriage. Without much working experience, it was very difficult for her to get a full-time job. Mandy ended up doing part-time jobs and had temporary employment. The unstable working hours and insufficient income created further stress for Mandy.

Apart from financial stress, Mandy's mental health deteriorated after her divorce. It was hard enough for her to face the divorce, not to mention the hurt she felt in being rejected by her father. These issues upset her immensely, and, as a result, for a period of time her mental health had been very poor, leading to a relapse and hospitalization. Upon discharge, she was referred by the social worker to live in a halfway house to assist her in her recovery and in getting back on her feet.

Concept and purpose of the technique

The Personal Strengths Assessment form is developed from a recovery perspective and is an essential and effective tool in recovery-oriented intervention. By using the form, the client is helped to review and take a fresh look at his/her personal experiences, and explore his/her potential strengths and skills.

SBCBT emphasizes the individuality of a client. The role of the worker is to work with the client in exploring his/her personal aspirations and goals and achieving them by utilizing his/her own strengths and abilities. The form is a comprehensive assessment of a client's strengths and expectations in recovery. Through it, the client is then able to identify and develop his/her internal and external strengths and resources in achieving those concrete goals. This chapter illustrates how the Personal Strengths Assessment form can be used to facilitate goal setting for Mandy.

The Personal Strengths Assessment form helps to explore seven aspects of a client's life, including: (1) living environment; (2) transportation and mobility; (3) financial and insurance; (4) work and education; (5) social support, intimate relationship, and religious belief; (6) health condition; and (7) leisure activities, talents, and skills. These aspects form the parameter for assessing a client's strengths and resources.

A timeframe of past, present, and future is set against the seven aspects of life of a client as mentioned above. In other words, in every aspect of life under the framework, the client would be asked about his/her current situation, his/her expectations and aspirations for the future, and previous attempts in achieving a particular aspect of his/her life.

Many clients find it hard to identify what resources they currently have. The supplementary questions suggested in the form combined with probing questions from the worker help the client scrutinize his/her life situation from a different perspective and thus, discover his/her strengths in recovery or goals for attainment.

In the section on personal expectations and aspirations, the client is helped to think through and write down, in the various aspects, what he/she wants to achieve in the future. This is useful for a client who has difficulties in setting goals. The client is helped to visualize the future and an ideal scenario. The worker then provides guidance for the client to define his/her goals in recovery and generate measures to mobilize the internal/external resources available to achieve those goals. Instead of being passively led by others (such as professionals), the client initiates the next step in achieving his/her goals.

When exploring previous efforts made by the client, the worker helps the client to identify resources he/she has had in the past. Some clients actually possess many skills before the onset of their illness. Due to illness, the clients may feel they can no longer reach the skill level they once had, and the skills may be forgotten over time. By exploring his/her previous attempts, a client can rediscover the strengths he/she once had.

Another important component of the SBCBT model is the instillation of hope. Hope for the future is a motivating force for ongoing recovery. The Personal Strengths Assessment form includes an index on hope to help the client examine his/her level of motivation in recovery.

Operation procedure

If time allows and the client is ready, the worker can consider going through the probing questions provided in the form item by item.

Part I helps the worker to understand the difficulties and challenges the client is currently facing and how these have impacted his/her life.

In Part II, the worker discusses with the client the seven aspects one by one. Some probing questions are suggested in each area to explore the client's strengths, ideal situation, and previous experiences. For example, in the area of living environment, the client will be asked what he/she feels are the most satisfactory and most unsatisfactory aspects. He/she will also be invited to describe what he/she considers to be an ideal living environment in order to examine his/her expectations and hopes.

Part III explores the internal strengths of the client as well as the social and community resources available.

After the client has described his/her aspirations in the different areas, in Part IV, the worker invites the client to choose three items he/she wishes to achieve most, what he/she can do to achieve the goals, and the barriers he/she may face in fulfilling those aspirations.

In Part V, the worker assesses the hope index of the client. For example, the client can examine whether he/she has the ability or means to change for the better, and evaluate his/her hopes and motivation to change.

The last part explores the receptivity of the client towards the various community resources. This gives the worker an idea of which resources the client is most willing to use.

Case illustration

Mandy did not like to write, so the worker went through the form with her verbally. In the discussion on living environment, Mandy mentioned that before she was admitted into the halfway house, she had to pay a high rent and had to work long hours in order to secure enough money to pay the rent. Work was her top priority in life; she felt she could not afford to have other distractions. Though her living environment had changed, her thinking pattern remained the same. In fact, Mandy had many negative emotions relating to work, but she did not know how to cope with them. She bottled them up and forced herself to go to work every day.

Mandy had not yet taken into account the fact that her circumstance had already changed. The rental pressure should no longer be an issue now that she was staying in a halfway house. On the other hand, the halfway house was an important resource for Mandy because it lessened her financial burdens. In fact, she could now attempt to re-prioritize her personal goals (e.g., working shorter hours with less salary), which would allow more mental space to deal with her emotions and also reduce her work stress.

Before Mandy moved to the halfway house, due to financial reasons, she had no choice but to rent subdivided units. Moreover, to contain her rental expenses, whenever a landlord increased her rent, Mandy moved to a cheaper place. Therefore, in those years after her divorce and before she was admitted into the halfway house, she moved from place to place. The financial pressure and the lack of stable living environment made her feel particularly sorry for herself. Filling out the Personal Strengths Assessment form had actually helped Mandy look at the situation from a new perspective (Table 3.1).

Table 3.1 Personal Strengths Assessment form[1] of Mandy

Personal Strengths Assessment form

Name (age): <u>Mandy (50)</u>

Note: This strengths-based recovery-oriented assessment tool serves as a reference for the worker. There may be no need for the worker to do assessment on every single aspect listed in the form.

For questions 2 to 8, if the client finds the item helpful in facing his/her life's challenges, please put an 'x' in the box provided.

I: Background information

---

1   What difficulties/challenges are you currently facing?

   <u>I have started a new job in April and felt stressed in my relationship with my senior</u>
   <u>who has bad temper.</u>

2   When did the difficulties/challenges begin?

   _____

3   In what way do the difficulties/challenges affect your life at the moment?

   <u>These have affected my mood and I feel quite unhappy at heart.</u>

4   On a scale of 0 to 10, where 0 means no impact at all and 10 means having great impact, how would you score the level of impact of those difficulties/challenges?

   _____

5   What measures have you been taking to resolve the difficulties/challenges? Are they effective?

   _____

6   Please give one example with which you can successfully resolve the difficulties/challenges:

   _____

7   What is (are) the reason(s) you have not continued using the problem-solving method?

   _____
   _____

II: Living environment

1	Where are you living at present? Are you living alone or with others?	☐
2	Which area in your current living environment are you satisfied with?	☐
3	Which area in your current living environment are you not satisfied with?	☐
4	Do you want to continue living in your current residence or do you want to move? Why?	☐
5	Please describe a place you have lived before with which you feel most satisfactory.	☐

(Continued)

Table 3.1 Personal Strengths Assessment form[1] of Mandy (*Continued*)

Current situation	Personal expectation and aspiration	Individual and social resources (previous attempts made)
Living in hostel where the rent is cheap and the environment is better than the subdivided unit	Able to apply for subsidized housing for singleton successfully	I used to live in a subdivided unit and the rental charge was around HK$5,000. I was helped by a social worker to move to a hostel for a singleton. The rent is cheap and I can have my personal space. My past experience taught me to be thankful for the opportunity to stay in a hostel.

III: Transportation, mobility

1	What means of transportation have you used before?	☐
2	What means of transportation have you used before but not now?	☐
3	Do you wish to expand your choices in means of transportation?	☐
4	If you could travel to anywhere you wish in the world, where would you like to go?	☐

Current situation	Personal expectation and aspiration	Individual and social resources (previous attempts made)
Currently working and living in Hong Kong Island and familiar with different communities.		Grew up in Ngau Tau Kok and Shatin District (i.e., two districts in Hong Kong)
High mobility, will go to different districts to meet friends during holidays.		Lived in Tai Po after marriage Went to church in Chai Wan

IV: Finance, insurance

1	What is your major source of income at present? What is your monthly salary?	☐
2	What are your basic expenditures each month?	☐
3	Based on your current financial situation, what changes do you wish to make?	☐
4	So far, when was the time you felt most satisfied with your own financial situation?	☐

Current situation	Personal expectation and aspiration	Individual and social resources (previous attempts made)
Have a stable job, earning around HK$9,000 per month. Receiving around HK$1,000 of Disability Allowance.	Have stable monthly income. Repay all debts. Able to save up some money for the tuition fee of the children.	Bought an insurance policy last year with around several tens of thousands of cash value. Have a small amount of stock.

(Continued)

Table 3.1 Personal Strengths Assessment form[1] of Mandy (*Continued*)

V. Employment, education

1   What is your current employment situation? Please describe your work environment and work nature. ☐
2   What does work mean to you? If you do not have a job now, do you want to find one? Why? ☐
3   Are you currently doing some activities that can help others as well as allow you to use your talents? ☐
4   What activities can bring you happiness, employment, and personal satisfaction? ☐
5   If you could create a perfect job for yourself, what would that be? Is it likely to be an outdoor or indoor one? A morning or a night job? Would it involve having overseas business trips? Would the job involve collaborating with others? Would the work environment be quiet or noisy? ☐
6   What is the job you have had that satisfied you most? ☐
7   Finding a job or staying in a job — which is more difficult for you? Why? ☐
8   Are you currently registered in any course to improve your knowledge and skills? ☐
9   Is there any area about which you would like to learn more? ☐
10   What is your highest educational attainment? What is your formal education experience? ☐
11   What is your view on going back to school to get a university degree, learning a new skill, or learning something just for fun? ☐
12   Do you enjoy teaching? Would you be interested in becoming a coach or a mentor for someone who needs help? ☐

Current situation	Personal expectation and aspiration	Individual and social resources (previous attempts made)
Currently working in a church, which is an environment I like. However, the boss has bad temper and it is very difficult to get along with him. Fortunately, other church members and colleagues are very supportive.	Would like to keep the present job and learn how to relate to my boss.	Had different work experiences including tour guide, bank clerk, and salesperson. Hold a security guard permit, and completed an activity assistant retraining programme.

VI: Social support, intimate relationship, and religious beliefs

1   What social and emotional support offered by your family will make you happy and feel good about yourself? ☐
2   Is there anything in your family relationship that you feel angry or unhappy about? ☐
3   What would you like to change in your family relationship? ☐
4   Where would you like to take a break and relax? Why do you like the place? ☐
5   What do you do when you feel lonely? ☐
6   Do you have a friend whom you can call, have a chat with, and hang around? If not, would you like to have one such friend? ☐
7   Do you yearn to have an intimate relationship with someone? Do you wish you had such a relationship? ☐

(*Continued*)

Table 3.1 Personal Strengths Assessment form[1] of Mandy (*Continued*)

8 Does religious belief mean anything to you? If it is important to you, what is your experience and how do you express your spiritual / religious side?	☐
9 Do you like nature?	☐
10 Do you like animals?	☐
11 Are you keeping any animal as companion at present? If not, would you like to keep one?	☐
12 Have you kept any animal as companion before?	☐

Current situation	Personal expectation and aspiration	Individual and social resources (previous attempts made)
Get support from church members and friends. My relatives also show concern, may have a meal together sometimes. At present, visit my father 2–3 times a year.	As a good witness for the Christian faith. Have a closer relationship with God.	Used my own experience in divorce to help others as a volunteer. Had poor family relationship. Being rejected by family members in times of need (i.e., divorce). Did not feel that the family could offer positive help and was unhappy at that time.

VII: Health condition

1 How would you describe your current health condition?	☐
2 Is having good health important to you? Why?	☐
3 Have you done anything to keep yourself healthy?	☐
4 What is your smoking habit?	☐
5 What is your drinking habit?	☐
6 What is your coffee drinking habit?	☐
7 What do you think are the impacts of smoking, alcohol, and coffee to your health?	☐
8 What medication(s) are you currently taking? Are they helpful to you?	☐
9 Generally speaking, how do you tell you are unwell physically? What can calm you down most if you are physically unwell?	☐
10 Have you experienced any health problem that has caused you some kind of limitation?	☐
11 In terms of health, is there anything you want or you need most?	☐

Current situation	Personal expectation and aspiration	Individual and social resources (previous attempts made)
Suffering from diabetes with high glycemic index, but the situation is under control.	GI remains normal. Able to control own emotions as these may affect my physical health.	Nurses at the hospital were considerate. They knew I did not have much money and often informed me if there were any health products on sale. They would also invite or make arrangements for me to join exercise groups.

(*Continued*)

Table 3.1 Personal Strengths Assessment form[1] of Mandy (*Continued*)

VIII. Leisure activities, talents, and skills

1　Name an activity that you enjoy doing, which leaves you feeling satisfied, ☐
　　peaceful, and competent.
2　Do you wish to participate more in those activities? ☐
3　What skills, abilities, and talents do you have (e.g., playing piano, writing poetry, ☐
　　dancing, singing, drawing, sense of humour, empathetic, kind at heart)?
4　What have you done in life that makes you feel proud of yourself? ☐
5　Is there anything you used to enjoy doing but have not done in a while? ☐
6　Among the activities mentioned above, is there one you would like to consider ☐
　　taking up again?

Current situation	Personal expectation and aspiration	Individual and social resources (previous attempts made)
Having meals and chatting with friends.	Going out on a trip with friends.	Enjoyed having a chat with others, and did not mind spending time as volunteer to help others.
Participating in halfway house activities.		

IX: Strengths

1　What characteristics do you have that make you strong and have helped you to overcome difficult times (e.g., positive attitudes, patience, sense of humour, work ethic, religious belief)?

　　Religion helps and it also changes me. I learn to be thankful and appreciate what I already have. Whenever I feel I am about to lose my temper, I try to keep cool by praying. Talking with social workers, friends, and other church members helps me reflect on my problems. I think what helps most is how to 'let go'.

2　What skills do you have?
3　What do you usually do in your leisure time?
4　Who are the people that have offered you help?
5　Who has helped you to maintain your physical health?
6　What are the good points about your current residence and its neighbourhood?
7　What makes your life purposeful and meaningful?

X: What are the three most meaningful aspirations/purposes in your life at present?

---

　i　Finish training in the halfway house and move to subsidized housing as soon as possible.
　ii　Maintain a job, have a stable income, and clear all the debts.
　iii　Learn to control emotions.
　　　1　What barriers do you have in achieving your objectives?
　　　2　What previous attempts have you made in achieving your objectives?
　　　3　What can you do now to help you achieve those objectives?

(*Continued*)

Table 3.1 Personal Strengths Assessment form[1] of Mandy (*Continued*)

XI: Assessment on level of hope

1 The client believes that there are things he/she is capable of doing to make things better.
high/**medium**/low
2 The client believes that he/she can find ways to make things better.
high/**medium**/low

XII: Assessment on factors affecting hope

Please use some time to think about your current life situation:	*1 = totally incorrect* *8 = totally correct*

1 When facing challenges, I will come up with many different ways to resolve the problem.
2 At present, I am actively pursuing my ideals.
3 There are many ways that I can resolve the problems I am now facing.
4 I feel that I am rather successful at present.
5 I can think of many different ways to achieve my current objectives.
6 I have now attained the objectives I set for myself.

XIII: In what way do you wish our services to be of assistance to you? What is the most appropriate service for you? What do you expect from the services we offer?

XIV: What type of community support services listed below would you consider participating in/ receiving?

housing	transportation	financial assistance	employment/work support
interest/activities	religious/spiritual support	school/education support	child care
self-care abilities	home management	basic community living skills	
health management	substance abuse		

Others: _____

1 When designing the Personal Strengths Assessment form, we made reference to a number of assessment tools, which included "Camberwell Assessment of Needs" (Slade et al., 2000), "Strength Assessment" (Rapp & Goscha, 2012), and "Person-Centered Strength Assessment" (Kisthardt, 2006).

While discussing the area concerning transportation and mobility, the worker suggested that, ironically, her frequent change of residence had probably given her great familiarity with various districts and had increased her knowledge about public transport. Mandy agreed and started to realize that from another angle, her unhappy past experience could turn into her strength instead.

Outcome

The Personal Strengths Assessment form helped Mandy identify her personal resources and strengths, sorted out the past, reviewed the present, and looked ahead to the future. The form also helped Mandy consider her priorities differently. She used to think that she had to devote all her time and energy to maintaining a job so that she could secure enough money for living expenses. The form helped her realize that she had a new resource, which was living in a halfway house, so that she could reallocate her energy and time to deal with her longstanding issue of lacking emotion–management skills in handling life stresses. She decided to set these as her new priorities so that she could learn the necessary skills to cope with work stress and interpersonal difficulties at work.

In addition, the form also helped Mandy identify her strengths and advantages. She liked to learn new ideas and skills (i.e., strengths). This became an area in which we could help Mandy raise her personal self-confidence. We encouraged her to enrol in courses to enhance and rebuild her work skills. From initially lacking self-confidence, Mandy gradually learned to make use of her own advantages in achieving her goals.

The focus of the Personal Strengths Assessment form is not on the client's difficulties, but on his/her abilities and strengths. Articulating the positives brings happiness and a sense of satisfaction for the client. Unlike working from a rehabilitation framework where the counselling session focuses on problems, the recovery model emphasizes the exploration of the client's strengths and available resources. It raises the client's awareness of his/her strengths and abilities instead of drilling onto difficulties and problems.

Reflection

Operationally, the form can be used flexibly according to the ability and the personality traits of the client. Clients who are more analytical and like to express themselves in writing can complete the form themselves. For clients who are not used to writing, the worker can facilitate the process by working through the form together, helping to detect available resources, and completing the form for them. However, even when the client completes the form him/herself, the worker still must conduct in-depth discussion with the client to make full use of the tool.

In addition, the worker has to be highly sensitive to the potential strengths and/or resources of which the client may not be aware. For a client who does not have a clear understanding of what is meant by 'resources', the worker can use probing questions to help him/her understand. For example, questions such as: 'Is this good or bad for you?' and 'Is this helpful?' may help. Some resources may not immediately come to mind for the client, so using more straightforward phrases such as 'good/bad' or 'helpful/not helpful' can help the client make the association.

Lastly, this form is an important tool in SBCBT for people recovering from mental illness. Not only does this form serve to instil hope and motivation and identify needs and aspirations of a client, it also facilitates the development of concrete goals in the recovery process. Concerning instilling hope and motivation, through the process of reviewing the form, the client is able to see what aspects of his/her life that he/she can potentially change and the strengths and resources that are available to him/her. These often become surprises that lead the client to see him/herself and the environment in a different and mostly positive light.

The worker tried to identify Mandy's interests and needs using the Personal Strengths Assessment form and helped her clarify her personal goals. In the employment/education section of the assessment form, the worker found out that Mandy had a lot of work experience and qualifications in different fields. The worker gradually noticed that Mandy was eager to learn and often registered in different courses. The worker then built on Mandy's interest in studying and invited her to participate in an emotion management group. The short-term goal for Mandy was to stay in the group until it finished and then, the worker devised a plan with Mandy to use what she had learned in order to achieve the objective of 'emotional management'.

Intervention tools: Emotional Thermometer, Situational Self-Analysis, and Thought Trap

Background information

Mrs. Ko was the only child in her family and was very much treasured by her parents. However, her father had to work long hours and was not able to spend much time with her. She was extremely close with her mother and she could remember clearly what she looked like, her smiles, anger, and every little detail.

Unfortunately, Mrs. Ko's parents died when she was still young. She was all alone in the world. Feeling sad, confused, and miserably helpless, she frequently thought of harming herself and following in her parents' footsteps. As time went on, she grew into a mature, independent, and strong woman. She got used to facing and solving life's challenges independently, set goals for herself, and tried hard to achieve them.

Many years later, she got married and had three children. Mrs. Ko became a full-time housewife while her husband earned a living to support the family. Mrs. Ko had to bring up her three kids on her own with little support from her husband. This was very stressful for her but her husband did not seem to share her feelings. He did not shoulder any responsibility in parenting and this was very upsetting for Mrs. Ko.

Mrs. Ko had no other relatives apart from her husband and children and she felt she had to face life's problems all by herself with no outside support. With time, Mrs. Ko's emotional heath was affected. She became easily angry when the children did not follow her instructions or when they did not pay attention in doing their homework. When she lost her temper, she would scold them or even use physical punishment. Her relationship with the children became tense. Coupled with her negative emotions, she lamented that this had greatly affected her children. They became even more rebellious and this further aggravated Mrs. Ko's bad temper. Gradually, Mrs. Ko noticed that she got depressed frequently, was in tears for no obvious reason, lacked volition, had persistent insomnia, and had thoughts of doing self-harm.

Fortunately, Mrs. Ko was able to contain her thoughts and was willing to seek help. She was later diagnosed with depression and was referred to the Integrated Community Centre for Mental Wellness for service.

Phase I of the recovery process

Maintaining hope and the motivation to change are key elements at the beginning of the recovery journey. It is necessary for the worker to help his/her client gain understanding of his/her current life difficulties and lead the client to see that there are ways out of his/her current situation. Consistent with any conventional cognitive behaviour therapy (CBT) approach, SBCBT uses a number of strategies and tools to help clients gain insight about how an interplay among their own physiological, emotional, cognitive, and behavioural response patterns may have contributed to their current life difficulties. Although this may seemingly look to be problem- or deficit-oriented, such awareness can (1) become a great motivation force for the client to decide to make change, and (2) point to some concrete areas where changes can be possible (i.e., identifying and setting goals). The strategies and tools include: Situational Self-Analysis exercise, Thought Trap, Emotion Thermometer, Physiological Response checklist, and Faces of Emotions.

Concept and purpose of the technique

The primary purpose of the Situational Self-Analysis exercise is to provide an effective tool to identify a client's physiological, emotional, cognitive, and behavioural response patterns when he/she encounters a specific life event relating to his/her life difficulties. It is particularly useful for understanding the interrelatedness among these responses and how they may have interacted to contribute to current life difficulties. The use of the Situational Self-Analysis exercise is often complemented by another CBT technique — Emotion Thermometer. The worker asks the client to give a score on his/her emotional status in the previous week, with 1 being the worst and 10 being

Table 3.2 Types of thought traps

Thought Trap	Description
1 Dichotomous thinking	Absolutist thinking. Things are seen as black and white, and have an absolute answer without other alternative explanation. People with this way of thinking consider that there is only 'yes' or 'no' or 'right' or 'wrong' answers, with no grey area in between.
2 Personalization	Putting the blame and responsibility onto him/herself when things go wrong.
3 Disqualifying the positive	Discounting successful experiences by attributing success to others' efforts. Personal successes are taken as luck with nothing to be proud of.
4 Catastrophizing	Magnifying the seriousness of the problem to a state of unamendable or unchangeable disaster.
5 Negative self-talk	Constantly criticizing and discouraging oneself when doing something, creating a very demoralizing spirit.
6 Arbitrary inference	Making negative conclusions without factual support.
7 Indecisiveness	Inability to make decisions but always having conflicting thoughts about the issues.
8 Emotional reasoning	Making judgments or drawing conclusions based on how one feels, without taking into account objective reality.
9 Blaming	Neglecting or shirking one's responsibilities, blaming others or bad luck.
10 Mind reading	Guessing the thoughts and motives behind others' gestures or behaviours (i.e., usually negative in nature).

Source: http://www.mindguide.hk/chi/psy2.php?product_id=1#.WroPoi5uZpg
https://www.ncbi.nlm.nih.gov/books/NBK470241/

the best. Through this technique, the worker can understand the current emotional status of the client and further explore the events behind the emotions with the Situational Self-Analysis exercise.

To enhance the client's awareness of his/her thought pattern that may be affecting him/herself, a tool describing ten common dysfunctional thought patterns (Table 3.2) has been developed (Beck, 2011). This tool helps the client identify his/her common automatic thought habits, understand how these thoughts are derived from his/her past life experiences, and relate these thought habits to the consequential undesirable emotional, interpersonal, and personal responses. The tool helps to improve the client's self-understanding and identify the core issues underlying his/her emotional disturbance.

Operational procedure

The worker would generally use a Situational Self-Analysis worksheet to help the client examine and understand the exercise more easily. The Self-Analysis

Table 3.3 Physiological response checklist

In your emotional ups and downs, have you ever experienced the following warning signals?		
Warning signal	*No*	*Yes*
Rapid heartbeat	☐	☐
Panic	☐	☐
Difficulty in breathing	☐	☐
Dryness of mouth/excessive salivation	☐	☐
Insomnia	☐	☐
Hot flush	☐	☐
Tensed muscles	☐	☐
Headache	☐	☐
Dizziness	☐	☐
Backache	☐	☐
Stiff neck and shoulder pain	☐	☐
Sweaty palms	☐	☐
Cold extremities	☐	☐
Stomach upset	☐	☐
Loss of appetite	☐	☐
Loss of concentration	☐	☐
Other: _____	☐	☐

worksheet should be as simple as possible (e.g., using diagrams and graphs). (See Appendix: Worksheet 01.) The incident shared by the client would be recorded briefly on the worksheet and the client would be invited to write down his/her physiological, emotional, cognitive, and behavioural responses. For a client who is not used to expressing his/her various responses, the worker would prepare supplementary tools such as a Physiological Response checklist (Table 3.3) and Faces of Emotions (Figure 3.1) to assist him/her in expressing his/her responses.

The worker should help the client identify all the emotional responses during a particular event and to indicate the intensity of each emotion with a score of 1 to 10. The purpose of this exercise is to examine dominant emotions. Then, the client would be helped to reflect on the automatic thoughts during that time. It is not easy for the client to identify the thoughts associated with the event. The worker has to use appropriate questioning skills to help the client to do so.

After the client has listed out his/her emotional responses and the thoughts behind an event, the worker would assist the client to examine the linkage between the automatic thoughts and the dominant emotions. The client is also helped to understand that different people could have different perceptions on the same event. Further, different perceptions could also bring about different emotional responses. The worker then introduces the ten common thought traps/cognitive distortions and uses the normalization

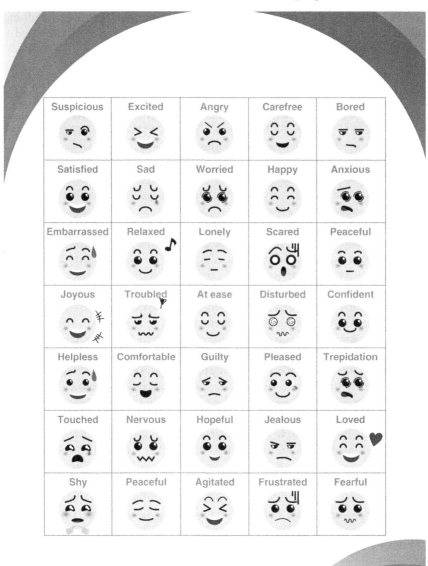

Figure 3.1 Faces of emotions.

technique to point out that everyone of us has some of these thought traps, and that the client is not 'abnormal'. The client is then helped to examine what cognitive distortion(s) he/she possesses and the negative emotions these may bring.

The worker would repeatedly provide guidance for the client in doing the Situational Self-Analysis exercise until the client is able to do it independently and his/her thought patterns can be identified.

Case example

Mrs. Ko was highly motivated because she loved her children and did not want them to be affected by her negative emotions. Furthermore, she wanted to improve her family relationship. However, she was not able to control her negative emotions and could not find any effective strategy to change them. She felt helpless and hopeless.

To instil hope for recovery, the worker reassured Mrs. Ko that emotional management was a skill that could be learned (i.e., normalization) and the first step to do so was to understand what contributed to her difficulties, in this case, uncontrollable negative emotions. Through the Situational Self-Analysis exercise, Mrs. Ko was helped to examine the interplay among her physiological, emotional, cognitive, and behavioural responses to various incidents in her life. The worker also explained to Mrs. Ko that our interpretation of events might be biased and could easily lead us to fall into our thought traps. The worker also explained to Mrs. Ko that we all have negative automatic thoughts (i.e., thought traps) when facing certain events in life and these negative automatic thoughts could trigger negative emotions. The worker told Mrs. Ko that changing our physiological, cognitive, and behavioural responses was the first step in changing our negative emotions. Furthermore, identifying personal thought traps was a key element in emotional management. When Mrs. Ko understood the mechanism behind her problem, she began to have hope in changing the situation.

In actual encounters with Mrs. Ko, the worker had used the Situational Self-Analysis exercise with her on numerous occasions in her recovery process. One example follows.

At one time, Mrs. Ko's son told his mother about his improvement in examination results. Her happiness in receiving news about the good academic performance of her son was soon overwhelmed by the anxiety brought about by the realization that another examination was coming soon. She was so worried that such concerns were prevailing even during her interview with the worker. The worker took this opportunity to conduct a Situational Self-Analysis exercise with Mrs. Ko.

The worker asked Mrs. Ko to recall her physiological responses at the moment when she realized that another examination was approaching. Mrs. Ko reported that she quickly developed a headache and she ranked the severity of her headache as 8 on a scale of 10. Emotionally, she ranked herself as level 8 in worries and level 9 in frustration. These high scores indicated the extent of the impact of her negative emotions on her physiological responses.

The thought underlying those responses of Mrs. Ko was that because of the good academic performance in that examination, her son would become too relaxed in his study due to arrogance and over-confidence. Consequently, her son would not be able to keep up with the good marks, his academic performance would fall behind, and he would not be able to enrol in a good school of their choice. Her son was not yet ten years old, but Mrs. Ko had already developed very strong catastrophizing thoughts about her son's future.

In terms of behavioural response, Mrs. Ko started to plan a study schedule for her son the very same day her son got the report, and she tried every tactic to push her son to study. Naturally, Mrs. Ko's son resisted. For Mrs. Ko, this resistance further proved that her son was not earnest and was inattentive in learning. Hence, her anxiety level got even higher (Figure 3.2).

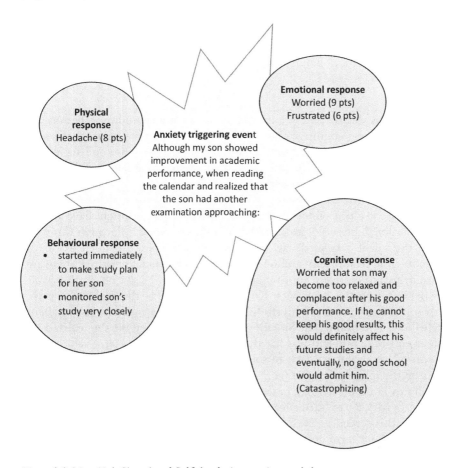

Figure 3.2 Mrs. Ko's Situational Self-Analysis exercise worksheet.

Table 3.4 Assessing my thought trap

Type of thought trap	Strongly agree	Agree	Neutral	Disagree	Strongly disagree
Dichotomous thinking					
Personalization					
Disqualifying the positive					
Catastrophizing					
Negative self-talk					
Arbitrary inference					
Indecisiveness					
Emotional reasoning					
Blaming					
Mind reading					

The worker further introduced the worksheet on the ten thought traps to Mrs. Ko (Table 3.4). She was able to grasp the concept very quickly and gained insight into how her thoughts could have an impact on her emotions. Mrs. Ko identified 'catastrophizing thought' as her own thought trap, which had led to her emotional distress.

Outcome

Mrs. Ko was able to benefit a lot from CBT strategies and tools because she had rather strong cognitive ability. Apart from her ability to grasp the techniques in conducting the Situational Self-Analysis exercise and to identify her own thought traps, she also trusted the worker and felt confident in the worker's capacity and her observations.

The use of the Situational Self-Analysis exercise in real-life experience facilitated the client's understanding of how her thought might have affected her emotional, physiological, and behavioural responses. Through this exercise, the client was made aware of the undesirable consequences on the parent–child relationship and on her personal emotional health. This awareness helped to motivate her to make changes.

Before using this tool, Mrs. Ko used to think that the problem was that her son was not serious in his study, not following her instructions, and being rebellious. After doing the Situational Self-Analysis exercise, she realized that the root of the problem was her dysfunctional thought pattern, which was a result of her prolonged lack of social support. Therefore, making the effort to stop disciplining her son (i.e., scolding and physically punishing him) and trying to build up a better parent–child relationship became the motivating forces for Mrs. Ko to learn effective emotion management and parenting skills. Indeed, this served as the primary goal in her recovery process. However, Mrs. Ko's long-term goal in recovery was to build up her own support network that could give her care and assistance in difficult times. For Mrs. Ko, the CBT tools not only instilled hope and motivation to change, they also played an important function in helping her set goals in her recovery process.

Reflection

To facilitate the recovery process of the client using the Situational Self-Analysis exercise and the worksheet to identify thought traps, it is important for the worker to take into consideration the cognitive ability of the client. Not every client is able to grasp the concepts as quickly as Mrs. Ko. The worker has to be clear and patient, providing guidance in a way that can be understood by the client. In the process of exploring and analyzing, the worker should try not to reveal the answers to the client. The client must think through the experience thoroughly to gain real insights.

Furthermore, the worker should also address the emotions of the client despite the fact that the analysis itself can be rather rational. The client should be given time and space to express his/her emotions and the worker should be receptive and open by showing understanding towards the client's emotions. Under the strength-based concepts, the worker should show ongoing sensitivity towards the strengths of the client and must give recognition to those strengths. Take the example of Mrs. Ko: during the process of self-exploration, the worker noticed her high cognitive ability, gave her sincere praise, and helped her to accept and appreciate her own strengths.

Conclusion

In the process of mental health recovery, instilling hope among people with mental illness is an important first step, but a difficult task to do. This chapter describe two sets of CBT strategies and tools that can potentially increase a client's awareness of his/her needs to make change, thus arousing his/her motivation and hope to do so. In the next two chapters, strategies and tools such as Dysfunctional and Functional Cycle Diagrams and the Life Priorities Game will be described in detail to further illustrate how a client's motivation and hope can be enhanced through SBCBT.

4 Phase II: Identifying needs

Introduction

This chapter describes Phase II of the strength-based cognitive behaviour therapy (SBCBT) recovery process, which involves need identification. Identifying needs is the first step towards setting goals for the client's recovery. The process helps the client to clarify what he/she wants to achieve and how he/she can go about doing this. It is of paramount importance for the client to be fully aware of and own the process when identifying his/her needs. After all, recovery is a personal journey that is directed by the client him/herself. In the case example that follows, we illustrate in detail how the Life Priorities Game and the Dysfunctional Cycle technique can be used to help the client to identify his/her needs.

Intervention tool: Life Priorities Game

Case background

Andy was 36 years old when the worker met him. He had his first onset of mental illness at the age of 22. The key symptom was auditory hallucination. Andy reported that the voices would criticize him, saying that he was worse than an animal, and that he should kill himself. He was very much troubled by the voices. Before Andy came to see the worker, he had been staying at home for three to four years.

Andy's psychotic symptoms emerged when he started working after graduating from high school (i.e., grade 13). He worked in a number of clerical positions, but none of the jobs lasted for more than several months because he felt he could not concentrate, was incapable of handling the nature of the work, and had poor relationships with his colleagues. Finally, he resigned from each job. At the onset of his illness, Andy had been working for more than three years. He was scared of the voices and felt that people on the street were laughing at him, taking special notice of him, and making accusations behind his back. He was hospitalized for a while at the age of 22, and since then, Andy kept going in and out of hospital, which was probably due to his poor drug compliance. As he claimed, he would stop taking medication on his own accord whenever he felt better himself. After Andy received services in the day hospital for some time, he was referred to the Integrated Community Centres for Mental Wellness for services so that he could participate in more social activities. The worker's first impression of Andy was that he was very quiet, passive, and lacked insight into what he wanted from life. It was easy to feel Andy's depressed mood when talking to him. He felt that he was incapable of doing anything, had a lot of negative emotions, felt that he was a failure, and did not believe that he could improve in any way. His auditory hallucination did improve with medication, though he still suffered from residual symptoms of hearing voices.

Phase II of Andy's recovery

Andy had no idea what he wanted to do in the centre when he first started the service. Due to his limited experience of successes in life, he had no motivation to change. In terms of his upbringing, Andy reported that he was born in a middle-class family and was living with his parents and an elder brother in a private housing estate. Both of his parents were professionals and were quite well-off financially. His elder brother, who moved out after marriage, graduated from a prestigious university and was a professional accountant. In comparison with his brother, Andy felt that he had done very poorly. According to Andy, his elder brother had been a bright student ever since he was a kid. They attended the same school and from Andy's perspective, his brother was the centre of attention both at home and at school. In fact, Andy's academic performance was comparable to that of his brother when he was in junior high and he also earned many commendations from the school. However, Andy started to feel stressful at school from around grade 8 onward. Andy had difficulties concentrating and his academic performance gradually declined. Even after two attempts, Andy still could not acquire high enough scores to meet the university's entrance requirements. He felt he was not as good as his brother and was utterly useless. In the end, Andy had to quit studying and got a job reluctantly. After around two to three years, Andy began to have doubts about his work ability and started to manifest auditory hallucination. He appeared to have no purpose in life and no motivation to change. Initially, the worker was not sure how to help him. Eventually, the worker decided to use the Life Priorities Game to help Andy identify his needs.

Concept and purpose of the technique

The primary purpose of the Life Priorities Game is to help the client examine the various aspects of his/her current life situation and ideal life situation. By comparing the differences, the client is then helped to identify goals and directions.

Table 4.1 Life Priorities Game of Andy

Imagine you have 1 million dollars for investment. Please distribute your investment to the various parameters by your 'ideal' life situation and your current 'actual' life situation.

	Parameter	Ideal investment (HK$)	Actual investment (HK$)
1	Work	300,000	
2	Spending time with spouse or boy/girl friend		
3	Spending time with family (parents, children, siblings)	200,000	550,000
4	Spending time with friends	200,000	100,000
5	Rest		
6	Entertainment		
7	On my own		
8	Physical activities	50,000	50,000
9	Pursuing personal interests	50,000	50,000
10	Further studies	50,000	
11	Keeping up with social trends or learning new things		
12	Participating in religious activities	150,000	250,000
	TOTAL	**1,000,000**	**1,000,000**

Operational procedure

The worker asks the client to complete a table comprising 12 life-related parameters including work, spousal relationship, family relationship, friendship, rest, entertainment, solitude, physiological activity, pursuing personal interest, further studies, keeping up with society or learning new things, and participating in religious activities (Table 4.1). The 12 life-related parameters are listed in the left hand column of Table 4.1. Two headings, actual investment and ideal investment, are labelled in the right hand columns. The client is then asked to imagine having 1 million dollars for investment. Under the column of 'actual investment', the client apportions the amounts he/she is investing in various real-life situations with a total amount not exceeding 1 million dollars. For instance, the amounts could be $400,000 in work and $300,000 in family life. Then, the client is asked to consider what amounts of the investment should be apportioned to different items in the Ideal Investment column. For example, in the parameter of 'spending time with friends', the client may put $150,000 as the actual investment and $250,000 as the ideal investment. The worker could then examine the differences between the client's 'actual' and 'ideal' life situations, helping him/her to explore his/her aspirations and goals and to develop plans in achieving them.

Case illustration

In examining the answers Andy gave to 'actual investments' in various items of the Life Priorities Game (Table 4.1), he put HK$550,000 on spending time with family members, HK$100,000 on spending time with friends,

HK$50,000 separately on physical exercise and pursuing personal interests, and HK$250,000 on religious activities. Andy explained that because he had nothing else to do, he stayed at home most of the time and spent a lot of time with his parents. He also loved to play with his nephew who came to visit them every week with his brother and sister-in-law. As a Protestant, Andy attended church every Sunday and was a member of the youth group at church. In general, Andy reported to have enjoyed those activities. For physical activities, Andy occasionally would go window shopping, hike, and play badminton with his friends at church. Andy was also interested in singing. He had participated in singing contests organized by youth centres and in the past.

In terms of his 'ideal investment', Andy wished to invest HK$300,000 in work, HK$200,000 in spending time with family members, increasing his time spent with friends from an investment of HK$100,000 to HK$200,000. For physical activities and personal development, the ideal investments remained the same as his actual situation (i.e., HK$50,000). He added HK$50,000 to further studies and reduced investment in religious activities to HK$150,000.

The worker then tried to explore the items in which Andy had increased the amount of investment in the 'ideal' situation (e.g., work). Andy explained that despite his worries about his capability to keep a job, he still wished he had stable employment. Andy told the worker that he was in his thirties and if he had a stable income, he could move out and live independently without financially relying on his parents. However, he did not have a clear idea on what he wanted to do career-wise. Andy had also added HK$100,000 in his investment to spend time with friends. According to Andy, he had very few friends, only two to three schoolmates from his primary and secondary schools with whom he would meet for a chat from time to time. Andy would like to spend more time with his friends from secondary school. However, as he did not do well at work and everyone seemed busy with their own lives, he had not kept in touch with these friends. In fact, he treasured these friendships. Andy was particularly close with a couple of friends who took badminton lessons together at school. At that time, Andy was very good at badminton. He represented the school in interschool competitions and had won many awards. These friends were precious to Andy and he wished to see them again. As for further studies, despite the unsuccessful attempts, he really wished to pursue university education. Andy wanted to become a professional but had no idea which field he would like to pursue.

The worker then discussed with Andy his priorities in areas in which he wished to increase his investment (i.e., work, friends, and further studies). Andy ranked spending time with friends as his top priority, followed by further studies, and then work. He felt that the reason for his lack of achievement at present was that he had no professional qualifications and therefore, he was not able to find a good job. As for friends, he felt bored with his life and wanted to rekindle friendships with his old friends. The worker then helped him to set short-term goals based on his priorities.

The primary purpose of this exercise was to work with Andy to examine his current life situation and compare it with his ideal situation. This could help him to build up new life goals and gave him motivation to take action for changing his life. Andy realized that he wanted to contact his badminton teammates from his secondary school again but worried that his friends might avoid him because of his illness. On exploration, the worker found that Andy still kept in touch with one of the teammates and knew that this group of friends would meet regularly to play badminton. The worker encouraged Andy to find out more about this activity and he was told that they would get together several times a year to play badminton and have a chat. With encouragement, Andy started to join their gatherings and met his closest friends. With this new development, Andy's social life improved.

Outcome

After working through the Life Priorities Games, Andy had a clearer idea on his life goals and what he wanted to achieve. This exercise helped Andy recall what he used to enjoy as a hobby and the strengths he had. Through this self-exploration and self-reflection of life priorities, Andy was able to set up goals and make action plans, paving the way to a more meaningful life and doing things he was interested in.

Reflection

In the Life Priorities Game, while the worker encourages the client to contemplate ideal life situations, the client might put too much focus on barriers and difficulties. The client may repeatedly make negative comments such as 'it is difficult to do so', or 'what's the point of talking about these ideals'. The worker has to show more empathy and encouragement to the client. When the client shows negative thoughts, the worker should keep reminding him/her of his/her motivating force—to make changes—emphasizing the need to let go of negative thoughts and unrealistic ideas.

Another point worth noting is that some clients might not have a clear numerical concept. Some people may have difficulties using money as a proxy to represent their life situations. The worker has to be patient and provide enough guidance to help the client complete the table. Some clients may have to put something down in every single box until every single item is filled in. Therefore, at the beginning, the worker has to point out that the client does not have to fill in every single item. He/she just needs to fill in items that he/she has either invested in their actual life situation and wishes to invest in their ideal life situation. The third point is that the client uses at least HK$50,000 (e.g., HK$50,000, HK$100,000) as a unit, rather than sums such as HK$5,000, HK$220,000, HK$230,000, and so on, the calculations are far easier.

Intervention tool: Dysfunctional Cycle

Case background

The background of this case, regarding Jenny, was described briefly in Chapter 2.

Phase II of Jenny's recovery

When Jenny first started her recovery process, she did not have much self-confidence, in particular, concerning her work situation. She was not sure if she had the capacity to do her job well and was often disturbed by the fear of a relapse. In fact, Jenny had very little knowledge on the issue of relapse, but in any case, did not feel she could manage it. To enable a more comprehensive understanding of her problems and the core issues, the worker used the Dysfunctional Cycle technique to help her identify her needs and changes that should be made. The Dysfunctional Cycle serves to identify needs and at the same time, motivate and instil hope for the client.

Concept and purpose of the technique

We can often get a glimpse of the problems of the client by examining mechanisms preceding the emotional distress — dysfunctional thoughts could lead to negative physiological, cognitive, and emotional responses that may then trigger negative behavioural responses. In turn, this may result in further negative responses or negative consequences from themselves or from others, and eventually, affect the client further. This chain of negative experiences is likely to appear repeatedly, reinforcing the negative thoughts and beliefs of the client, and develop into a vicious cycle.

Clients are usually not aware of how the vicious cycle begins and the mechanism behind it. The task of the worker is to help the client reveal the 'invisible' vicious cycle by drawing it out and making it easier to understand. In addition, actually putting it down on paper can make an even deeper impression on the client. The Dysfunctional Cycle technique helps the client to understand the negative consequences of his/her usual response pattern and to explore ways to break the cycle. Achieving a different outcome requires the client to take different action. The Dysfunctional Cycle technique allows the client to consider alternative responses, motivates him/her to change, and explores possible action to redress the current situation.

Operational procedure

Drawing a Dysfunctional Cycle Diagram can be considered a next step following a Situational Self-Analysis exercise. As described in the previous chapter, the Situational Self-Analysis exercise examines an event in the daily life of the client, which has triggered his/her negative emotions. It helps to analyze the client's physiological, cognitive, and emotional responses to the event, and then the client describes his/her behavioural reaction. In addition to focusing on how emotions may be affected by a person's thinking, by drawing the Dysfunctional Cycle, the client also can examine the consequences of his/her behaviour on him/herself and on others, and in what way these responses contributed to worsening the situation. In gist, the client is helped to review details of the incident to complete the Dysfunctional Cycle in full.

After completing the Dysfunctional Cycle Diagram, the worker analyzes the diagram in detail with the client. The client should be given ample time to study the diagram and make his/her own observations and interpretations before the worker enriches the discussion with his/her supplementary feedback. The worker will then work with the client to explore strategies to break the vicious cycle, providing guidance for the client to see a way out.

Another way to apply the technique of Dysfunctional Cycle is to consolidate insights on the series of Situational Self-Analysis exercises conducted by the client. After working repeatedly on the exercise, the client is helped to understand the reason(s) contributing to the persistence, or even worsening, of his/her problem. Take the case of anxiety: affected by past experiences, when the client encounters a threat, he/she tends to exaggerate the risk and underestimate his/her own capacity to cope, and concludes that he/she is unable to deal with the situation. The vicious cycle becomes:

> Occurrence of a triggering event → automatic negative thoughts → physiological discomfort and anxious emotion triggered by the negative thoughts → client becomes even more worried and anxious → adopts avoiding/safety behaviours for self-protection → client therefore is not able to test out his/her ability to cope or verify if the situation is as threatening as he/she has imagined → further reinforces the beliefs that he/she is not capable

With this technique, the Functional Cycle is often used in parallel with the Dysfunctional Cycle — though Functional Cycle is often used at a later stage of the intervention process. When the client is gradually able to grasp effective strategies to stop the vicious cycle, naturally, some positive consequence will occur. It would then be a good time for the client to work out the Functional Cycle. This can help the client identify his/her changing pattern, gain insight through the changes, and explore the critical moments in his/her self-development.

Case illustration

Jenny shared the most stressful and worrying event she experienced recently in one of the sessions. It was when she started a new job and her boss briefed

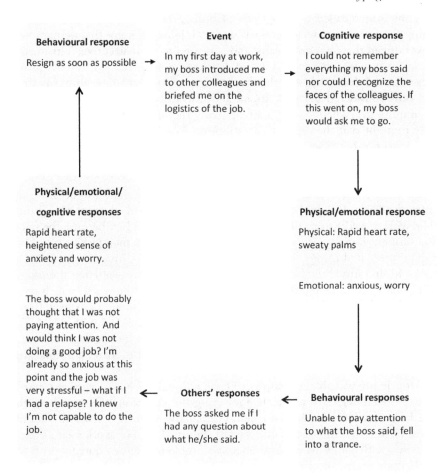

Behavioural response

Resign as soon as possible →

Event

In my first day at work, my boss introduced me to other colleagues and briefed me on the logistics of the job.

→

Cognitive response

I could not remember everything my boss said nor could I recognize the faces of the colleagues. If this went on, my boss would ask me to go.

Physical/emotional/cognitive responses

Rapid heart rate, heightened sense of anxiety and worry.

The boss would probably thought that I was not paying attention. And would think I was not doing a good job? I'm already so anxious at this point and the job was very stressful – what if I had a relapse? I knew I'm not capable to do the job.

Physical/emotional response

Physical: Rapid heart rate, sweaty palms

Emotional: anxious, worry

Others' responses

The boss asked me if I had any question about what he/she said.

←

Behavioural responses

Unable to pay attention to what the boss said, fell into a trance.

Figure 4.1 Dysfunctional Cycle of Jenny.

her on the first day at work. The worker talked with Jenny to explore her physiological, emotional, and cognitive responses. Physiologically, Jenny experienced a rapid heart rate and sweaty palms. Emotionally, she felt extremely tense and worried. In terms of her thoughts, Jenny recalled that she kept thinking she would not be able to remember what her boss said and was not capable of fulfilling the tasks (Figure 4.1).

In previous sessions when the concept of Thought Trap was introduced, Jenny realized that it was easy for her to fall into the trap of catastrophizing, and she would experience the associated physiological and emotional responses. The worker went on to help Jenny explore her behavioural responses. She described herself as extremely worried and scared, and she became physically frozen and her mind went blank. The only thing she could think of was to run away from the situation.

Jenny also recalled the reactions of others. Her boss immediately asked Jenny again if she understood what was said. Jenny thought that perhaps her boss noticed that she went blank and appeared to be inattentive. This made Jenny even more nervous and scared, her heart rate quickened, and her muscles stiffened. Jenny fell into the thought trap of mind reading, thinking that her boss considered her slow to act and not up to par. Jenny then became even more overwhelmed by catastrophizing the situation that her boss probably thought that she did not pay attention to what he/she said and would decide to fire her. She thought 'I am already so overwhelmed with anxiety now. With this job being so stressful, I could easily get a relapse. This is not a suitable job for me and I should quit!'.

To raise Jenny's awareness on how her past experience might have an impact, the worker used the technique of Metaphor to illustrate the point. The worker told a story of someone who threw away a box because the person thought it contained a snake. In fact, the box contained just a rope. The rope represented things that Jenny was capable of handling; the image of a snake hiding inside the box was similar to Jenny's catastrophizing thoughts. The worker commented that Jenny tended to imagine the worst, which created a lot of unnecessary fear in herself, and as a result, she just ran away from situations. In reality, this could be something she could deal with easily. To make a deeper impression on Jenny, apart from working through the idea verbally, the worker gave her a real box as a reminder to avoid falling again into a similar thought trap.

After Jenny was able to grasp her Dysfunctional Cycle, the worker started to explore strategies to make changes using the Functional Cycle. Through the Functional Cycle Diagram, Jenny gradually identified what she could do to change and the way to go forward (Figure 4.2). The worker continued to work with Jenny to explore effective problem-solving strategies and to build up her sense of competence. The original goals set by Jenny served as a motivating force to help her sustain her efforts.

Outcome

By drawing the Dysfunctional Cycle Diagram, Jenny was able to have a comprehensive understanding of what contributed to her anxiety and the interrelationship among various factors. These insights gave Jenny a stronger sense of control over the situation. The worker then helped her to analyze further and she understood that:

1 She tended to fall into the thought traps of catastrophizing and mind reading, and she got herself trapped in the negative emotion of anxiety. In fact, the reality was often not as bad as she imagined.
2 Her behavioural responses would affect the sequence of events and subsequently, escalated her anxious emotion.

3 Her pattern of quitting the job to get out of the situation had, in fact, taken away her opportunity to demonstrate what abilities she possessed. This had further enforced an inaccurate image of herself as being incapable. In gist, she had never had a chance to understand her real ability in an objective manner.

4 Her current need was to break the vicious cycle.

5 She could choose alternative response actions to break the vicious cycle.

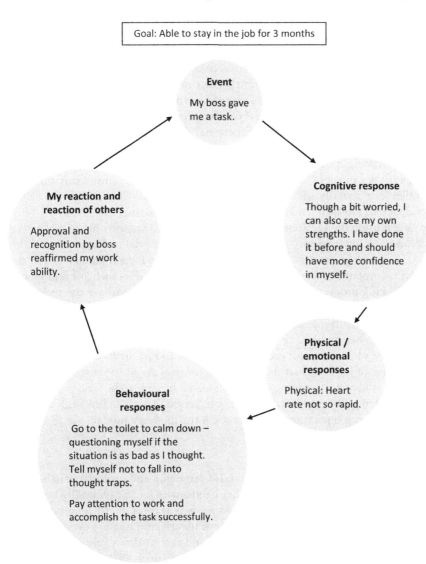

Figure 4.2 Functional Cycle of Jenny.

In the next phase of Jenny's recovery, the goals she set for herself were to overcome her anxiety by breaking the vicious cycle, enhance her sense of competence by trying something new, and increase her confidence through successful practical experiences. Later, she found a job and her short-term goal was to stay in it for at least three months (i.e., the probationary period). Eventually, she was able to achieve her goals and to break away from the pattern of quitting the job immediately to get away from anxiety-provoking situations. Jenny became a formal employee after probation.

Reflection

In the case of Jenny, it is highly appropriate for the worker to use the technique of Metaphor together with the Dysfunctional Cycle. For clients who cannot recall in detail what has happened or those with relatively little insight into their own situation, the use of Metaphor can highlight the core issue. Similar to the technique of Dysfunctional Cycle, the use of Metaphor helps to clearly define a relatively abstract idea as a visual diagram or concrete image, making it easier to understand. When these two techniques are combined, they can supplement each other. For instance, in Jenny's situation, the worker can actually give her a box (or something) to remind Jenny of her tendency to fall into the thought trap of catastrophizing.

When using the Dysfunctional Cycle Diagram, the worker has to pay special attention to the tendency of the client to try to personalize the problem. This is very common, because when going through the Dysfunctional Cycle, the client is constantly asked to examine his/her inadequacies such as blind spot in the thinking process and problem areas. The worker has to use the technique of normalization regularly to prevent the client from putting all the blame onto him/herself, thinking that the problem was caused by his/her inadequacies, and it is his/her own doing in worsening the situation. Therefore, the worker has to give a lot of encouragement to the client and reaffirm the client's ability. In the case of Jenny, when she shared her worries about the first day at work, the worker kept encouraging her and validated her strengths. The purpose was to enable Jenny to learn how to appreciate herself. This is in line with the concept of utilizing one's internal resources in the recovery model.

Conclusion

In this chapter, we highlighted two CBT strategies and tools that can be used to facilitate a client to identify his/her needs, which can potentially be translated into goals in the recovery process. It is important to remember that the client is the director of the process of identifying his/her needs (indeed, throughout the entire recovery process) and the worker's role is to help the client to achieve the tasks at every stage of the process. When the client feels that he/she is in control of the process, he/she will be more motivated to achieve the goals and will in the end attain the state of a liberated self.

5 Phase III: Formulating and developing goals

Introduction

To achieve what the client wants in life, Phase III focuses on setting goals based on the needs identified in Phase II. However, for many recovering individuals, it can be a challenge to uncover purpose and meaning in living. Many are more concerned about managing their illness and medications; others simply give up, not caring what hopes and meaning in life might bring to them. In this phase, the most important component is to help the client develop meaningful goals for living. Two useful strategies and tools are the Life Goal Formulation Chart and Pie Chart, and they will be illustrated through two case examples.

Intervention tool: Life Goal Formulation Chart

Case background

The background information of Andy is described in Chapter 4.

Phase III of Andy's recovery

In the previous chapter, we described how the Life Priorities Game helped Andy in identifying three goals for recovery: (1) to expand his social circle by reconnecting with his high school peers, (2) to pursue further studies, and (3) to find a job and become independent of his parents. This section illustrates the technique for developing an action plan using the Life Goal Formulation Chart.

Concept and purpose of the technique

The Life Goal Formulation Chart aims to help the client formulate a clear and concrete action plan to achieve his/her goals in recovery. To ensure a successful experience, goals of the action plan must be feasible and the proposed tasks need to match the capacity of the client.

Operational procedure

The client is invited to set priorities among goals he/she has set for recovery using the Life Goal Formulation Chart worksheet (Table 5.1), and write down the reasons for his/her selections and rankings. The worker then explores the possible action plans, specific tasks, outcome indicators, and dates of completion for each of the goals set by the client. An important part of the worksheet is to decide what reward/incentive the client can give to him/herself when a goal is achieved. This is very useful in sustaining the continuous efforts of the client.

Case illustration

The goal Andy considered as top priority was to reconnect with his badminton teammates and to join their gatherings. He wanted to accomplish this goal in two months' time. In terms of self-reward, Andy considered the experiences of spending time with his old teammates, having a chat, and sharing a meal with them as concrete incentives in and of themselves. In addition, Andy wanted to rejoin the youth centre choir, which he had stopped attending for one to two years. Again, he wanted to achieve this in two months' time. Because the choir was an open group, Andy's plan was to go there regularly and learn different types of songs. For self-reward, Andy felt that as long as he was able to put the plan into action, it was already a reward.

For the second goal, Andy recognized that it was not practical for him to go back to college and get a diploma. He mentioned clerical jobs could be one prospect for him, especially those in accounting. In terms of action plan, Andy decided to enrol in an accounting course as a first step and then possibly progress to learning clerical skills such as Excel and Chinese and English word-processing, which generally took nine months to one year to complete. Finances were not a concern for Andy, as his family would support him to pursue his studies. For self-reward, Andy stated that he would seek his family's support to go for a short trip to Thailand.

The third goal of Andy was to get a stable income. Andy decided to work on it later when he could achieve the first two goals because his family members did not put too much pressure on him in this aspect. As long as he took steps to pursue his studies, his family members would be happy and worry-free.

Outcome

Andy had been very cooperative in the process. Indeed, he was rather fortunate as he was well-accepted by his high school badminton friends. When he reconnected with his classmates, they were happy to rebuild friendships with him. Andy enjoyed spending time with them when they met several times a year.

Table 5.1 Andy's Life Goal Formulation Chart

My priorities in life goals
1st: The goal I would like to achieve most.
5th: No harm if not able to achieve.

Priority	Life goal	Reason
First	Broaden my circle of friends	1 Used to enjoy spending time with friends. 2 Feel happier, do not have to stay home all day.
Second	Pursue further studies	Hope to acquire vocational skills that help with future employment.
Third	Find a stable job	Hope to find a stable and more permanent job. Do not want to rely on parents financially and in daily life.
		Hope to be able to live independently in the future.
Fourth		
Fifth		

My goals

Goal	Concrete plan
Goal 1: Broaden the friends' network	1 Contact ex-badminton teammates and join their gatherings. 2 Join the singing class organized by a youth centre (client had not participated in the singing class for some time).
Goal 2: Pursue further studies: targeted at clerical job	1 Take courses in basic accounting. 2 Take computer courses (Excel, Publisher, Chinese and English word-processing).
Goal 3: Do not want to make concrete plan yet to find a job at present	

My concrete plans to achieve the goals

Goal	Concrete plan	Success indicator	Timeframe	Self-reward
Goal 1: Broaden the friends' network	Contact ex-badminton teammates and join their gatherings.	Make attempts in the next two months and join gatherings of ex-classmates.	nil	Not necessary
	Join singing group at youth centre (have not participated for a while).	Go back to the youth centre and enrol.	nil	Not necessary
Goal 2: Pursue further studies: targeted at clerical job	1 Take courses in basic accounting. 2 Take computer courses (Excel, Publisher, Chinese and English word-processing).	Participate in the various training classes.	Six to nine months	Not necessary
Goal 3: Do not want to make concrete plan to find a job at present			Pending until completion of the first two objectives	

What made Andy even happier was that his ex-classmates treated him as 'normal' despite his mental illness. They did not hold any prejudice against him. As for joining the singing class at the youth centre where Andy was once a member, Andy noticed that the class size was small and the number of participants was very unstable. He also felt that he might not be able to get along well with the people in the group. Although Andy originally wanted to expand his friendship circles by joining activities outside of the church environment, he finally decided to rejoin the church choir because he enjoyed singing a lot and he did not think the youth centre choir matched his expectations.

For further studies, Andy started to join accounting courses and his interest in the subject increased. The worker provided Andy with more resources on relevant courses and encouraged him to try. Andy eventually enrolled in a work-rehabilitation programme that involved training participants in different trades, including office work. Through the programme, Andy was able to learn clerical and computer skills such as accounting, word processing, and Excel. He was also able to practice these skills at the centre on a daily basis. After training in the centre for half a year, he was recommended to do workplace attachment. With practice experience, Andy was later ready to find a job.

Reflection

Some clients may find it challenging to formulate concrete plans to achieve their goals, and it may be easier if they can work on the goals one by one. In addition, some clients may need more time to work out concrete plans. For this kind of client, the worker may need to spend more time and give more guidance to them. In Andy's case, the worker had to provide information on relevant courses to help Andy achieve his goal of future studies. Because it is very likely for a client to experience many difficulties and barriers in achieving his/her goals, it is very important to offer continuous encouragement to the client and assess the situation with him/her on a regular basis so that the action plans and tasks can be modified quickly when necessary to ensure success and/or positive experiences for the client.

Furthermore, the worker has to help the client identify his/her internal and external barriers. Internal barriers could be undesirable lifestyle, behaviours, and negative emotions. External barriers generally refer to environmental factors, financial reasons, and inadequate resources in the community. The worker needs to help the client find ways to overcome the barriers. This will be discussed in detail in the following chapter.

Intervention tool: Pie Chart

Apple was in her forties and was diagnosed with manic depression when she was at college in the Mainland. At that time, she was emotionally disturbed by her relationship with the opposite sex and regularly had to seek medical consultation at the hospital.

Years later, Apple had her own family and a daughter. Despite the changes in her life circumstances, she was still troubled by her emotional distress. Apple's husband had to travel between Hong Kong and the Mainland constantly due to work. They had a lot of conflicts and their relationship was far from harmonious. Apple put all her attention on her only child who was then at high school. She wanted to play the role of an excellent mother, providing the best for her daughter and grooming her into a talented person.

Due to work stress and tension in her marital relationship, Apple's mental condition had not been stable and she experienced multiple relapses. In 2008, she started receiving psychiatric treatment in Hong Kong. She had insomnia and other manifested symptoms such as compulsive buying. After a period of treatment, she became more stable emotionally. Upon discharge from the hospital, she was referred to the Integrated Community Centre for Mental Wellness for recovery-oriented intervention service.

Phase III of Apple's recovery

When the worker first met Apple, her goal was to improve her emotional problems for fear of affecting her daughter. She was eager to be a good mother.

Apple was easily agitated and annoyed. Whenever she felt things did not go as smoothly as she wished, she would immediately lose her temper and lambast others. At work, due to her bad temper, she did not get along well with colleagues. Similarly, at home, she vented her anger easily and had poor relationships with family members.

Apple often felt annoyed about her daughter's living habits, which she thought were untidy and disorganized. Whenever Apple noticed her daughter's untidy behaviours, she would immediately feel irritated and start scolding her. At the same time, she also recognized similar behavioural patterns in herself — easily agitated, not very reliable, leaving things about, inattentive in studying, and so on. To a certain extent, Apple's irritation with her daughter was partly due to her own messiness in life. She thought her daughter had learned from her poor habits and that she had been a bad influence on her. Apple reckoned that she was not a good role model for her daughter and wanted very much to change the situation. Therefore, one of her goals was to become a good mother.

Although Apple attached great importance to her daughter's education, she was not sure what she should do next. Furthermore, the goal of being a good mother for her daughter was too broad and vague. To explore what made a good mother in Apple's perception, the worker used the Pie Chart technique.

Concept and purpose of the technique

When a client has certain vague ideas or ambiguous values needing clarification, or when he/she has some fixed idea of a certain thing or concept, but is unable to see other perspectives or possibilities, the Pie Chart serves to be a useful technique to broaden the client's thinking, to stimulate new inspiration, and to explore information that may go unnoticed. With a broader perspective, the client may assess a situation in a different light, taking on more information before making a judgment or decision. By articulating an idea in concrete terms, composing the Pie Chart, and assessing the relative proportion of different components, the client is helped to reflect more deeply on the issue involved.

The advantage of using the Pie Chart instead of listing out individual items is that the Pie Chart also allows a graphic display of the relative weight of each item, highlighting their differences and making it easier to make comparisons. This can help to examine the situation in a more comprehensive, objective, and concrete manner.

During the process, apart from paraphrasing the thinking of the client, the worker can also provide additional information for the client's reference. This is particularly useful for clients with limited knowledge on a topic. The worker can help to educate the client and facilitate a more in-depth discussion on the subject. Take the example of Apple: As she could list out only two to three characteristics of a good mother, the worker provided information on what people in general considered to be qualities of a good mother. This broadened her perspective and enabled a more in-depth examination of Apple's ideas on good motherhood.

Operational procedure

The first step is to invite the client to describe his/her thoughts about the topic and list out what it may be comprised of. In the process, the worker can offer further suggestions for the client to broaden his/her perspective. The next step is to invite the client to evaluate each proposed item or component within the Pie Chart and assign relative importance by using percentages. After completing the chart, the worker would explore with the client whether the exercise has given him/her any new insights or inspired different views.

Case illustration

To clarify Apple's ideas on what constituted a good mother, the worker used the Pie Chart technique. The criteria of a good mother listed by Apple were:

1 to provide the child(ren) with good education (i.e., financially sound);
2 to provide support and be with them throughout their development, and help them to develop good living habits;
3 to teach them how to think and be morally sound; and
4 to provide a good learning environment (i.e., setting a good example in keeping the home tidy and emotionally calm).
5 to maintain emotional stablility.

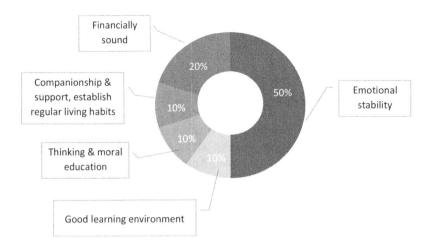

Essential qualities of a good mother

Figure 5.1 Apple's Pie Chart.

In terms of the relative importance of various items, Apple assigned 50% to emotional stability; 20% to financial condition; 10% to companionship, support, and regular living habits; 10% to thinking and moral education; and 10% to learning environment.

After completing the Pie Chart (Figure 5.1), it became clearer to Apple that, from her perspective, emotional management was the most important quality of a good mother and this then became her primary goal in recovery.

Outcome

Initially, Apple had a list of items she wished to accomplish and considered each and every one of them equally important. She had no idea how and where to start and there was no way she could work on all the items at the same time. In the process of completing the Pie Chart, Apple realized that her own emotional healthiness was vital to the development of her daughter (occupying 50% of all the items), and this helped her to prioritize her goals.

Helping Apple to identify her core goal did not intend to deny the importance of other items. This technique helped Apple to think through all the items and to understand more deeply what she wanted for herself. It also facilitated her to set priorities, keep focused, and make plans that were feasible and practical.

Apple was committed to her plan for recovery after the goal setting. Her cognitive ability was good and she was highly capable of reflecting on how her emotion was affected by her thinking process. She not only benefited from the sessions with the worker, but she was also eager to learn on her own.

After some time, her relationships with both her daughter and colleagues had improved.

Reflection

At the beginning, Apple had only a vague idea of the potential negative impact of her emotion on her daughter. With increased understanding and knowledge, her motivation to work on improving her emotional management skills increased. The most significant motivator was her wish to provide an environment for her daughter's healthy development. Before, Apple's life revolved around her daughter and she paid very little attention to her own needs. Through the various exercises, Apple was able to broaden her perspective from focusing on immediate issues such as her daughter's education needs, being a good mother, and family relationships, to those related to her own emotional health. When she started to pay attention to improving her emotional management skills, her entire recovery focuses shifted, resulting in a change in priorities in life concerns.

Conclusion

Setting concrete goals is an important step in the recovery process and paves the way for the development and fulfilment of the goals. The Life Goal Formulation Chart and Pie Chart, which are often used in conventional cognitive behaviour therapy (CBT) intervention, can also be used for developing strength-based oriented goals in our strength-based cognitive behaviour therapy (SBCBT) approach. During the process, the worker must have a good understanding of the needs, aspirations, and strengths of the client in order to facilitate him/her to develop concrete, achievable, and individually tailored goals. Moreover, the worker has to develop a strength lens in order to steer the client towards a strength-based approach in mental health recovery.

6 Phase IV: Exploring internal strengths and external resources

Introduction

After goal setting, in Phase IV, the worker's task is to explore the client's internal and external resources. In many cases, clients are not aware of their own capacity; some may have forgotten the potentials and abilities they once possessed or are unaware of useful resources available in their networks or in the community. Therefore, the worker has to help the client continuously to explore both his/her internal and external resources and raise his/her awareness of his/her own capacity to build a new, meaningful, and fruitful life.

Using two case examples, this chapter intends to illustrate how the Personal Strengths Assessment form, the Life Review Exercise, and other strategies in identifying community resources can be used to help a client discover his/her internal strengths and external resources in the recovery process. In applying these techniques, it is critical to engage the active participation of the client rather than directly providing them with information. Furthermore, the client may have other concerns that stop them from using the resources, and it is the worker's role to identify those barriers and find out ways to overcome those difficulties.

Intervention tool: Personal Strengths Assessment Form

Case background

Annie was first known to us when she was in her fifties. After divorcing her husband ten years ago, she moved back to her maiden home and lived with her parents who were in their eighties. Annie had an elder brother and a younger sister, both of whom moved out after getting married.

Since childhood, Annie felt that her parents had never paid much attention to her. In her view, they seemed to care only for her brother and sister, particularly her brother. Being the eldest son, her brother had to give up studying at an early age to support the family. Out of guilt, Annie's mother cherished him most and he was allowed to make all major family decisions. Annie's sister, on the other hand, was very clever, had excellent academic performance, and had a successful career. She was the daughter who made the family proud. Being the middle child, Annie felt neglected. For that reason, even at a very young age, Annie was eager to have her own family and wanted to leave home as soon as she could. Eventually, she married a foreigner and settled abroad. They had a son.

She was first diagnosed with schizophrenia in 2000 when she was still abroad. At that time, she often felt she was treated poorly by her husband. Annie also had poor relationships with her in-laws. Whenever Annie had a conflict with her mother-in-law, her husband always sided with his mother and offered Annie no support. Annie felt deeply hurt by her husband's behaviour. Under these circumstances, Annie started to experience emotional and mental problems. She heard voices accusing her of being useless. She also heard voices asking her to die, and little things in her surroundings could trigger her suicidal ideations. For instance, while waiting for traffic lights, Annie would have an impulse to dash into the road; or she visualized hanging herself when seeing rope-like items. All these were highly disturbing for Annie.

Eventually, Annie was admitted into the hospital for treatment. Moreover, her marriage was also in crisis. Annie felt that her husband was not there to care for her and support her when she needed him most. She felt that he just did not care. He even took a trip to Europe without notifying her, leaving her alone with her mother-in-law with whom she could not get along. This was unbearable for her and she then decided to buy herself an airline ticket and return to Hong Kong. Her husband just ignored her, and Annie lost all hope of reconciliation. She felt her husband was heartless for not taking into account their years of marriage. Finally, Annie decided she wanted a divorce.

Annie lived with her parents after divorcing her husband. Although she was the only one staying with her parents, she still could not let go of the feeling of being unloved and neglected. She still felt that they loved her siblings more. Tension started to build up. Minor incidents such as the kindness shown when her mother talked to her brother or the little gifts her mother gave to the grandchildren were all sources of unhappiness for Annie.

Annie's mental status was not stable after she came back to Hong Kong. She still had symptoms of schizophrenia. She was then referred by the community nurse of the hospital for regular counselling with the social worker at the Integrated Community Centre for Mental Wellness.

Phase IV of Annie's recovery

At the early stage of Annie's recovery process, the focus of the worker was to help Annie find ways of dealing with her symptoms and identifying factors affecting her mental instability. At that time, she had auditory hallucinations and suicidal ideation. Annie reported that at times, she would feel extremely gloomy and could not help but scream out loud at home. Annie always stayed at home and seldom went out; therefore, her condition was known only to her family members. Nonetheless, her mother was very worried.

From what Annie shared about her background, it was obvious that her self-confidence was very low. In her maiden home, she believed that her status was low and her view was insignificant. In terms of intelligence and achievement, she was also the lowest. Annie had never been gainfully employed. From her perspective, she was a useless person because she did not do well academically, had no earning power, and at middle age had to move in with her parents due to her failed marriage. All these 'failures' created a very negative self-image.

As Annie's mental state was unstable, the initial task of the worker was to help Annie stabilize her symptoms. From a recovery perspective, it is important that the client learn to take responsibility to manage his/her own physical and psychological health, reduce or minimize the symptoms, and cope with the limitations brought about by the illness. Therefore, it is necessary for the client to be equipped with knowledge about the illness and its symptoms. In this regard, Annie realized that her condition was very much influenced by the quality of her sleep. Whenever she had insomnia or had not had sufficient rest, various psychotic symptoms appeared.

Eventually, Annie's condition became more stable and she no longer experienced auditory hallucination. Then, the worker started to work on her aspirations and goals. Her first goal in recovery was emotional stability and to become symptom-free. Her second goal was the health of her parents, and the third was for her son to be successful in his career. After reviewing her goals, the worker clarified with Annie that her second and third goals were, in fact, beyond her control. Annie then adjusted the second goal to learning how to take care of her parents. Similarly, Annie could do very little to achieve the third goal because her son was still abroad. Annie then decided to put aside the third goal for the time being.

However, on a practical level, Annie insisted that she was not capable of taking care of her parents. She felt that she could not even shoulder the responsibility of taking her parents to attend medical follow-ups. At that point, it was her elder brother who assumed most of the responsibilities in taking care of their parents. He visited them often and took them out for various activities. Therefore, Annie did not feel confident at all to achieve her goal of learning how to take care of her parents. Initially, she was also not motivated to even attempt some of the suggestions discussed in the counselling sessions.

To identify Annie's strengths, increase her motivation, and to raise her sense of competence and confidence, the worker used the Personal Strengths Assessment form with Annie.

Concept and purpose of the technique

In strength-based recovery-oriented intervention, identifying clients' strengths is an essential step, and the Personal Strengths Assessment form is an important tool during the process. After setting goals in Phase III, it is necessary for the client to discover what internal strengths and/or external resources he/she possesses that can help with his/her goal attainment. Please refer to Chapter 3 for the structure and contents of the Personal Strengths Assessment form.

Personal resources can be internal or external. External resources refer to resources that are available in the client's surroundings/network that he/she can use to facilitate goal attainment. These may include community facilities, family relationships, social networks, and so on. Internal resources refer to the client's own strengths, including positive personality traits, knowledge, skills, talents, abilities, specialties, interests, academic qualifications, experiences, religion, and so on. The Personal Strengths Assessment form helps to identify all internal and external resources of the client comprehensively.

In this chapter, the case of Annie is used to illustrate the application of the Personal Strengths Assessment form and how the resources identified are used to facilitate goal attainment for the client.

Operational procedure

As this form is very comprehensive, the worker may not be able to cover all the areas in one interview. If feasible, the client should fill in the information him/herself; for those not capable of doing so, the worker should collaborate with the client to complete the form in the first few interviews.

Case illustration

The form completed by Annie is illustrated in Table 6.1. The worker discussed the aspects of the form with Annie one by one.

In the area of living environment, Annie felt that as compared with living space abroad, the environment in Hong Kong was much more crowded. However, she also realized that it was not feasible for her to have more personal space as she was staying in her maiden home. The worker then tried to explore if there was anything she liked better in the environment. Annie stated that whenever she wanted some peace and quiet moments, she would visit the little fountain in the park downstairs. The sound of the water comforted her and calmed her down. Therefore, this fountain had become a precious resource for her. As one of the goals of Annie was to learn ways of taking care of her parents, the worker suggested that she could make use of this community resource and take her parents for a stroll in the park. Annie agreed to try.

In the form, Annie also mentioned a market near the place she lived. Upon exploration, she agreed that living abroad, though more spacious, was less convenient; in Hong Kong, it was very convenient to go shopping and do other activities. In other words, this assessment form has widened her perspective, she no longer saw her life only from a negative light.

In the area of transportation and mobility, considering that the public transportation network in Hong Kong was highly advanced and convenient,

Table 6.1 Personal Strengths Assessment form of Annie

Personal Strengths Assessment Form

Name/age of client: <u>Annie/54</u>

Note: This strength-based recovery-oriented assessment tool serves as a reference for the worker. There is no need for the worker to do assessment on every single area listed in the form.

For questions 2 to 8, if the client finds the item helpful in facing his/her life's challenges, please put an 'x' in the box provided.

I: Background information

1　What difficulties/challenges are you currently facing?

　　<u>Emotional instability/auditory hallucination</u>

2　When did the difficulties/challenges begin?

　　<u>Since onset of illness in 2000</u>

3　In what way do the difficulties/challenges affect your life at the moment?

　　<u>Symptoms appear with inadequate rest. For example, a voice criticizing me for being useless, and no one would listen to me. Sometimes, when feeling restless, I would scream out loud at home. And this is worrying for family members.</u>

4　On a scale of 0 to 10, where 0 means no impact at all and 10 means having great impact, how would you score the level of impact of those difficulties/challenges?

　　<u>7</u>

5　What measures have you been taking to resolve the difficulties/challenges? Are they effective?

　　<u>I would talk to the staff in the centre.</u>

　　<u>When feeling restless, irritable, and having insomnia, I would go for follow-up earlier/find comfort in prayers.</u>

6　Please give one example with which you can successfully resolve the difficulties/challenges:

　　<u>Once, my mother made special arrangements to have tea with my brother after he came back from abroad, and she kept serving him tea. I felt that my mother had never been so kind to me. So I prayed silently, hoping to calm myself down.</u>

7　What is (are) the reason(s) you have not continued using the problem-solving method?

　　<u>I might not be able to find the centre worker or get an earlier appointment immediately whenever I need to.</u>

(Continued)

Table 6.1 Personal Strengths Assessment form of Annie (*Continued*)

II: Living environment

		living with family members
1	Where are you living at present? Are you living alone or with others?	
2	Which area in your current living environment are you satisfied with?	☐
3	Which area in your current living environment are you not satisfied with?	☐
4	Do you want to continue living in your current residence or do you want to move? Why?	☐
5	Please describe a place you have lived before with which you feel most satisfactory.	☐

Current situation	Personal expectation and aspiration	Individual and social resources (previous attempts made)
- Living with family members - Skills in doing household chores - Have a stable residence - A water fountain in the park downstairs - A market (price is cheap)	- Spacious and renovated living environment - Have more personal space	- Had lived abroad

III: Transportation, mobility

1	What means of transportation have you used before?	☐
2	What means of transportation have you used before but not now?	☐
3	Do you wish to expand your choices in means of transportation?	☐
4	If you could travel to anywhere you wish in the world, where would you like to go?	☐

Current situation	Personal expectation and aspiration	Individual and social resources (previous attempts made)
- Convenient public transport - Eligible for the $2 concessionary fare	- Able to take parents for medical follow-up appointments - Know how to take parents to brother's place - Opportunity to visit son in Australia	- Driving

IV: Finance, insurance

1	What is your major source of income at present? What is your monthly salary?	☐
2	What are your basic expenditures each month?	☐
3	Based on you current financial situation, what changes do you wish to make?	☐
4	So far, when was the time you felt most satisfied with your own financial situation?	☐

(*Continued*)

Table 6.1 Personal Strengths Assessment form of Annie (*Continued*)

Current situation	Personal expectation and aspiration	Individual and social resources (previous attempts made)
- Disability allowance (around $3,000) - Savings	- Enough would do (around $4,000) - Medical expenses are likely to increase in the future, and need to take care of family members	- Housekeeping money - Small amount of stock

V: Employment, education

1 What is your current employment situation? Please describe your work environment and work nature. ☐
2 What does work mean to you? If you do not have a job now, do you want to find one? Why? ☐
3 Are you currently doing some activities that can help others as well as allow you to use your talent? ☐
4 What activities can bring you happiness, employment, and personal satisfaction? ☐
5 If you could create a perfect job for yourself, what would that be? Is it likely to be an outdoor or indoor one? A morning or a night job? Would it involve having overseas business trips? Would the job involve collaborating with others? Would the work environment be quiet or noisy? ☐
6 What is the job you have had that satisfied you most? ☐
7 Finding a job or staying in a job — which is more difficult for you? Why? ☐
8 Are you currently registered in any course to improve your knowledge and skills? ☐
9 Is there anything area about which you would like to learn more? ☐
10 What is your highest educational attainment? What is your formal education experience? ☐
11 What is your view on going back to school to get a university degree, learning a new skill, or learning something just for fun? ☐
12 Do you enjoy teaching? Would you be interested in becoming a coach or a mentor for someone who needs help? ☐

Current situation	Personal expectation and aspiration	Individual and social resources (previous attempts made)
- I need to take care of my parents and with the income from the disability allowance, there is no immediate need to get a job.		- Had working experience as a clerk before marriage.

VI: Social support, intimate relationship, and religious beliefs

1 What social and emotional support offered by your family will make you happy and feel good about yourself? ☐
2 Is there anything in your family relationship that you feel angry or unhappy about? ☐
3 What would you like to change in your family relationship? ☐

(*Continued*)

Table 6.1 Personal Strengths Assessment form of Annie (*Continued*)

4 Where would you like to take a break and relax? Why do you like the place? ☐
5 What do you do when you feel lonely? ☐
6 Do you have a friend with whom you can call, have a chat, and hang
   around? If not, would you like to have one such friend? ☐
7 Do you yearn to have an intimate relationship with someone? Do you wish
   you had such a relationship? ☐
8 Does religious belief mean anything to you? If it is important to you, what is
   your experience and how do you express your spiritual / religious side? ☐
9 Do you like nature? ☐
10 Do you like animals? ☐
11 Are you keeping any animal as companion at present? If not, would you like
   to keep one? ☐
12 Have you kept any animal as companion before? ☐

Current situation	Personal expectation and aspiration	Individual and social resources (previous attempts made)
- Protestant, attends church regularly and does volunteer work - Regular meeting with two close friends at secondary school - Contacts son via long-distance telephone calls every day	- Prayers help to calm down emotions - Religion makes me feel loved	- Used to tell husband about things that happened in life - Had attended church before but changed denomination for a more convenient place of worship

VII: Health condition

1 How would you describe your current health condition? ☐
2 Is having good health important to you? Why? ☐
3 Have you done anything to keep yourself healthy? ☐
4 What is your smoking habit? ☐
5 What is your drinking habit? ☐
6 What is your coffee drinking habit? ☐
7 What do you think are the impacts of smoking, alcohol, and coffee to your
   health? ☐
8 What medication(s) are you currently taking? Are they helpful to you? ☐
9 Generally speaking, how do you tell you are unwell physically? What can
   calm you down most if you are physically unwell? ☐
10 Have you experienced any health problem that has caused you some kind of
   limitation? ☐
11 In terms of health, is there anything you want or you need most? ☐

Current situation	Personal expectation and aspiration	Individual and social resources (previous attempts made)
- Regular follow-up at psychiatric clinic and good drug compliance - Fix appointment to attend advanced follow-up consultation when needed	- Getting good quality sleep - Emotionally stable	- Contact the social worker or community nurse whenever experiencing auditory hallucination - Regular follow-up and compliance to medication

(*Continued*)

Table 6.1 Personal Strengths Assessment form of Annie (*Continued*)

VIII: Leisure activities, talents, and skills

1 Name an activity that you enjoy doing, which leaves you feeling satisfied, ☐
   peaceful, and competent.
2 Do you wish to participate more in those activities? ☐
3 What skills, abilities, and talents do you have (e.g., playing piano, writing ☐
   poetry, dancing, singing, drawing, sense of humour, empathetic, kind
   at heart)?
4 What have you done in life that makes you feel proud of yourself? ☐
5 Is there anything you used to enjoy doing but have not done in a while? ☐
6 Among the activities mentioned above, is there one you would like to ☐
   consider taking up again?

Current situation	Personal expectation and aspiration	Individual and social resources (previous attempts made)
- Joining the ink painting class and the Chinese calligraphy class organized by the centre	- Continue with these activities with the aim of calming oneself and obtaining support	- Watched movie - Watched television - Prepared meals

IX: Strengths

1 What characteristics do you have that make you strong and have helped you to
   overcome difficult times (e.g., positive attitudes, patience, sense of humour, work
   ethic, religious belief)?

   - Willing to sacrifice for the family, dedicated to family

   - Patience, a good listener

   - Kind-hearted, willing to help others

   - Know how to respect others

   - Religious belief: the love of God enables me to become stronger during hardship

2 What skills do you have?

   - Do household chores and prepare meals

3 What do you usually do in your leisure time?

   - Watch movies/watch TV/attend ink painting class/attend Chinese calligraphy class

4 Who are the people that have offered you help?

   - Family members/secondary school classmates/psychiatrists/community nurse/
   social workers/other inpatients in the hospital

5 Who has helped you to maintain your physical health?

   - Myself/psychiatrist/community nurse/social worker

(*Continued*)

Table 6.1 Personal Strengths Assessment form of Annie (*Continued*)

---

6   What are the good points about your current residence and its neighbourhood?

- The water fountain in the park/the market

7   What makes your life purposeful and meaningful?

- My son can grow up healthily, becomes an accomplished person

- Spend time together with family members as parents are getting old

- Stay healthy physically and emotionally

X: What are the three most meaningful aspirations/purposes in your life at present?

---

i   Maintain emotional stability
ii Learn how to take care of parents
iii _____

1   What barriers do you have in achieving your objectives?

- Symptoms would appear without sufficient rest

- Parents not understanding my situation

- Restrict by physical condition and not able to go farther

2   What previous attempts have you made in achieving your objectives?

- Attended regular follow-up consultations

- Complied with medication

3   What can you do now to help you achieve those objectives?

- Instil hope in life, increase motivation

- Manage my symptoms better

- Learn caring skills and acquire health information for my parents and myself

---

XI: Assessment on level of hope

---

1   The client believes that there are things he/she is capable of doing to make things better.

high/**medium**/low

2   The client believes that he/she can find ways to make things better.

high/**medium**/low

(*Continued*)

Table 6.1 Personal Strengths Assessment form of Annie (*Continued*)

XII: Assessment on factors affecting hope

Please use some time to think about your current life situation:	1 = totally incorrect 8 = totally correct
1 When facing challenges, I will come up with many different ways to resolve the problem.	6
2 At present, I am actively pursuing my ideals.	6
3 There are many ways that I can use to resolve the problems I am now facing.	6
4 I feel that I am rather successful at present.	4
5 I can think of many different ways to achieve my current objectives.	5
6 I have now attained the objectives I set for myself.	4

XIII: In what way do you wish our services to be of assistance to you? What is the most appropriate service for you? What do you expect from the services we offer?

- Regular interviews and support to me
- The ink painting class and the Chinese calligraphy class organized by the centre
- Health information (e.g., talks and workshops)

XIV: What type of community support services listed below would you consider participating in/receiving?

housing	transportation	financial assistance	employment/work support
Interest/activities	religious/spiritual support	school/education support	child care
self-care abilities	home management	basic community living skills	
health management	substance abuse		

Others: _____

Note: The internal resources of Annie included respect for others, patience, willing to listen and offer help, loves her family, dedicated, willing to make sacrifices, and cautious about giving criticisms. These attributes not only helped her in raising an excellent child in the past, they also helped in maintaining her friendships. These internal strengths, together with resources in the community, could facilitate her in achieving the goal of taking care of her parents.

the worker explored the possibility of Annie taking her parents to attend medical follow-ups, or just taking them to her brother's home. Eventually, Annie recognized that she had both the knowledge and the skills to accomplish the task. Her knowledge of the transportation network enhanced her sense of competence in achieving this goal.

Annie's situations in social support, intimate relationships, and religion were areas the worker spent most time on exploring with her. Annie was a Protestant and she attended church activities regularly. She was eager to volunteer her time in doing some odd jobs at the church. She was very religious, was committed to her faith, and found it helpful to pray to God. Annie alleged that the love of God could make her strong, and her faith supported her in times of difficulties. Her church life also allowed her the opportunity to have a regular social life and to receive support from other church members.

In the area of friendship, Annie only had a small circle of friends. The closest were two secondary school classmates. They had a close relationship and had been keeping in touch all along — either by phone or would meet up occasionally. These two friends knew her situation well, including her mental illness and divorce experience. They were very supportive. When Annie was unhappy, she would find these two friends to have a chat. Sometimes, they would go to see a movie together as a distraction from her negative feelings. Annie started to realize the significance of their friendship. Not only did this give her continuous support, but it was also an outlet for her to vent her stress. The worker helped her realize that she placed a high value on friendship, and she would do what she could to sustain the relationships.

With regard to her health condition, the primary concern of Annie was the management of her mental illness. Annie reported that she attended follow-ups regularly and had good drug compliance. From this information, the worker helped Annie identify her internal strengths, including having good insight into her illness, and trusting the helping professionals such as the psychiatrists, nurses, and social workers. She was motivated to seek help. In addition, the worker pointed out the knowledge Annie already had regarding her illness (e.g., an awareness of signs and symptoms of her mental instability such as auditory hallucination and knowledge on how and when to seek help). She was also aware of the quality of sleep being an important warning signal for her mental instability. When her condition was not stable, Annie took initiative to contact the social worker or the community nurse, or simply made an earlier follow-up appointment. These measures helped her a lot in managing her illness and well-being.

On leisure activities, talents, and skills, Annie reported that apart from attending church, she was not a very active person. She used to like drawing and apart from that, she did not have any particular interest. The worker suggested that because the Integrated Community Centre for Mental Wellness also offered interest classes, she could take advantage of this as one of the community resources that could help her develop her interests and talents. Eventually, Annie joined the ink painting and Chinese calligraphy classes offered by the centre.

When the worker explored with Annie what she felt most proud of in life, she said her son was definitely the centre of her attention. Using this as an entry point, the worker started to explore Annie's internal resources. When Annie described some of the positive characteristics of her son (e.g., well-behaved, learned in earnest, showing filial obedience), Annie realized that she did well as a parent. She was proud of her parenting skills and felt that she had brought up a brilliant child. On exploration, Annie expressed that as a mother, she was cautious with criticisms, was always a good listener, did not interrupt when her son was speaking, and did not criticize him easily. She cared for him a lot but at the same time, allowed him much freedom. Though staying abroad, her son called her long-distance on a nearly daily basis. Their relationship was very close indeed.

The worker then explored further Annie's other personal attributes. She described herself as someone who loved her family, and who was dedicated and willing to sacrifice for her family. She was also patient, willing to listen to others, kind-hearted, knew how to respect others, and was willing to offer help. Because of these positive characteristics, her friends were willing to talk to her and she was able to maintain long-term friendships. This realization was new to Annie. She now knew that being a good listener and being considerate were attributes not everyone had. She started to appreciate herself more.

Outcome

Annie used to consider herself useless and her past experiences were full of failures, constraints, and shortcomings. It was only after Annie had completed the form that she started to realize the resources available around her. More importantly, she rediscovered her positive attributes and internal strengths and started to acknowledge the many resources she possessed.

The usefulness of the form was particularly noticeable when the worker discussed with Annie her proud feelings towards her son. By examining the situation from a different light, from just being a proud mother, Annie began to appreciate how good she was in her parenting skills. It was also obvious from the discussion that Annie was happy and full of confidence in describing her relationship with her son, which was markedly different from her narration of her own upbringing. When Annie was able to recognize her internal strengths of being a successful mother with good parenting skills, she was more at ease when relating to and taking care of her own parents. Annie realized that by identifying and understanding her internal strengths and external resources, she could make use of them in achieving her goals.

The worker realized that with the increased understanding and recognition of her own strengths and abilities, Annie's self-esteem was enhanced and her motivation to change increased. The worker had also tried to encourage Annie to use her internal strengths in achieving her goals. For example, the ethos of selfless dedication in her religious belief enabled her to take care of her parents and family members whole-heartedly without being too calculative. Indeed, Annie could also make good use of her interpersonal skills to relate to her parents and family members, learning how to allow for her own needs while also taking care of them.

In terms of external resources, apart from the water fountain in the park, her knowledge of the transportation network was also an asset. Annie used to shift the responsibility of taking care of her parents to her brother, saying that she did not know the ways around. After completing the assessment form, Annie realized that it was not as difficult as she thought. The availability of external resources that Annie had identified encouraged her to take action. In recognizing her strengths, Annie became more hopeful, felt more competent and more confident in moving forward in the road to recovery. Annie believed that with the possession of those resources, she was able to accomplish her goals.

Reflection

The Personal Strengths Assessment form is a detailed and all-encompassing tool, which takes considerable time in discussing and completing the contents. It requires patience from both the worker and the client. In general, the design and format of the assessment form is conducive to helping the client in gaining insight about him/herself. Without actually writing down the points, the discussion on strengths can be vague and non-specific. The guidelines provided are very thorough and clients are often pleasantly surprised at the strengths and/or resources they already have.

Clients are often not aware of the potentials of small things in their surroundings. Sometimes, the client may not take in the worker's perspective as he/she may think that the worker is overly enthusiastic to appease him/her, or fail to put down anything because no 'real' strengths can be identified. The worker has to instil the idea that the term 'personal strengths' does not only refer to the commonly accepted attributes such as having a pretty face, high academic qualifications, professional knowledge, or intelligence; strengths can be anything the person can make use of within and around him/herself. The client may deny having any internal strength and it is the worker's job to make use of the real-life experiences of the client (i.e., mentioned by the client or observed by the worker in the interview processes) to remind him/her of and reaffirm his/her strengths.

We all have unique strengths, experiences, aspirations, and needs. By completing the Personal Strengths Assessment form, the client is helped to have a thorough understanding of him/herself, with which he/she can take the lead in formulating his/her own recovery plan and go forward with confidence, hope, and a sense of competence.

Intervention tool: *Life Review Exercise*

Case background

The case background of Andy is described in Chapter 4.

Phase IV of Andy's recovery

At this stage, Andy had already reconnected with his ex-badminton team-mates. They had gatherings and he would play a badminton game or two with them. At the same time, the worker also noticed the low self-esteem of Andy and considered his future very gloomy indeed.

Concept and purpose of the technique

The purpose of this technique is to examine the various stages in the client's development and explore what he/she has achieved in those developmental stages. Specifically, the client is asked to recall events at different stages of his/her life (childhood, adolescence, adulthood, old age) that he/she has felt particularly happy about or has provided a sense of accomplishment. In each life stage, the client is invited to write down a few success stories. After completing the form, the worker explores with the client what abilities or strengths he/she has behind those success stories.

Operational procedure

The Life Review Exercise features four columns for the client to fill out his/her major life events during childhood, adolescence, adulthood, and old age. The client is encouraged to put down significant life events in each column (see Worksheet 03). The worker then discusses each entry in detail with the client by encouraging him/her to elaborate on his/her experiences. At the same time, the worker facilitates the client to explore what internal resources and/or external resources the client has in making the experience a success. After thorough exploration, the worker helps the client summarize his/her strengths and resources that are present in him/herself.

Case illustration

In recalling his childhood experiences, Andy reported that when he was in grade 2, he was praised by the teacher for his talent in singing and was invited to sing in front of the class. This created a deep impression on him. Andy told the worker that as a child, he was often praised for his good singing voice; however, his parents did not see singing as a career that could earn a living, and did not encourage him to pursue in that path. The worker then asked Andy whether he considered singing an interest that could make him happy. Andy positively confirmed that this was indeed his interest and that was the reason why he tried to join the singing group in the youth centre. He said he might also consider joining similar activities such as those affiliated with the church or organized by other agencies. That said, Andy stated that his current priority was to find a stable job and developing his interest in singing was not his immediate concern. The worker then asked Andy again why the teacher praised him for his singing, and whether or not he would consider having a good voice a personal strength of his.

In recalling important events during adolescence, Andy remembered once, a classmate sprained his ankle during a school trip and Andy volunteered to stay behind to help and accompanied the classmate to a hospital (i.e., in the presence of a teaching staff). This incident made Andy felt very satisfied and happy. When asked what this incident meant for Andy, he told the worker that he learned that he was a caring person and had the ability to withstand hardship (because it was a laborious process with a sense of responsibility to assist the limping classmate to go to the hospital). He felt that people should help each other, but as he grew up, he became hesitant in offering and seeking help to and from others.

Another incident Andy recalled was a camping trip with several secondary school classmates. They planned to camp for two nights. Unfortunately, the first day, it started to rain heavily and the tent was soaking wet. What was worse was the fact that they lost their way. This was an unforgettable event for Andy as they were able to find the way through the mountain and arrived home safely despite the challenges. The worker asked what he learned about his ability from this event. Andy replied that he realized he had the ability to solve problems in difficult times. In particular, when they went the wrong way, it was Andy who led the group back on track. For Andy, the lesson he learned was that if people helped each other, they could solve many problems. This was a treasurable experience for him, as the group of friends he camped with were also his badminton teammates.

Andy mentioned another incident about an inter-school badminton tournament. His team won the first runner-up for the group competition, and he ranked sixth in the individual competition himself. Andy stated that this was his prime time before he was 16 years old. He described himself to be an assiduous and diligent person, and he was able to make efforts in meeting challenges and achieving his goals. However, at that time, his family members did not approve of his enthusiasm in playing badminton. Andy stated that were it not for his perseverance and persistence, he might not be able to do what he had accomplished and derive satisfaction from it. He felt that his perseverance had helped him a lot.

Interestingly, Andy failed to put down any significant event after he was age 17. On exploration, Andy explained that since the onset of his illness, his life seemed to have gone stagnant. Since then, he felt useless and did not harbour any hope in life. Therefore, there was nothing to record in his adulthood. The worker persisted by encouraging Andy to review this part of his life carefully to examine if there was anything worth noting during that period. Andy eventually revealed that at age 26, when he was idling at home, feeling bored and unhappy, he ignored family members' advice and went to Taiwan for two weeks. He felt very relaxed during the trip and was not so depressed after he returned. The worker then asked Andy to use this incident to reflect on his strengths. Andy told the worker that he felt he had no choice at that time. He was just bored and wanted to get away from his parents for some time. However, he mentioned that this was the first time he had ever gone on a trip on his own without his parents. Moreover, he said he had arranged everything well and smoothly on his own.

From Andy's description, it looked as though Andy was a problem solver and could resolve his own problems as a child and adolescent. But as he grew older, other circumstances, like his inability to keep a job due to illness, made him feel useless and worthless. While acknowledging his difficulties, the worker also kept reminding him of the areas he was good at. To make a deeper impression, a checklist of all the strengths he had mentioned was prepared, which included having a good voice, not afraid of hardship, trying to meet challenges in life, being perseverant, and having good planning skills. Andy was then invited to go through the checklist and was helped to realize that despite his current feelings of worthlessness, to the contrary, he used to be/ and could be a capable person with many strengths and resources (Table 6.2).

Outcome

Although Andy might not be able to make changes in a short period of time, through this exercise, he was able to examine his strengths and resources from a different angle and this helped him restore a bit of his self-image. In addition, the checklist generated could also serve as a reminder on the resources he possessed in achieving his goals. Lastly, the worker had also collected information/evidence of Andy's successful experiences, which could be used to remind Andy of his abilities in the future. (Called the Piggy Bank technique, this will be described in detail in Chapter 9.)

Reflection

Some clients tend to recall negative experiences when doing the Life Review Exercise. The worker has to state very clearly the purpose of the exercise is to record positive, successful, and happy experiences. Experiences that may not be very positive (or neutral) but are considered by the client as making deep impressions can also be recorded. The worker will then help the client examine alternative interpretations of the event (i.e., focusing on how the event illuminates the positive characteristics and abilities of the client). To achieve this, the worker needs to have good sensitivity.

On the other hand, some clients may claim that they cannot recall any relevant events nor any successful experiences. They see themselves as useless and have nothing worth sharing. When this happens, the worker should explore with the client to see if his/her negative feelings are so overwhelming that they affect his recall of any positive experience. However, the worker needs to be mindful that if the client is not able to think of any positive incident, the worker should not push the client. After completing the exercise, the worker has to help the client summarize and make sense of his/her experiences.

Table 6.2 Life Review Exercise

Please recall events at your different life stages that impress you as happy or successful and record them in the table below.

Childhood	*Adolescence*	*Adulthood*	*Old age*
Event 1 - In grade 2 (7 years old), my teacher complimented me on my beautiful voice and invited me to sing in front of the class.	Event 1 - At 15, I encountered some potentially dangerous situations while camping with my classmates but was able to resolve it. In the end, everyone arrived home safe.	Event 1 - Not able to think of any at the beginning because I had not achieved much after 17. - I started to idle at home at the age of 26 but felt bored and went to Taiwan for around two weeks by myself. And it was a good feeling.	Event 1
Underlying meaning - I enjoyed singing but could not make it into a career. But I can still sing as an interest. - I am good at something and totally useless, I guess.	Underlying meaning - I have the ability to solve problems. - Although I may not be able to find a solution on my own, with some help from others, I can still do it.	Underlying meaning - I can do something for myself when I feel depressed and the outcome was satisfactory. - This was the first time I took a trip on my own. I have the ability to make plans and take action.	
Event 2 - In primary school, I volunteered to help a classmate who was injured during a school outing. - I helped to support him and accompanied him to the hospital.	Event 2 - At 16, my team was the first runner-up at the inter-school badminton tournament, and I ranked sixth in the individual competition.	Event 2	Event 2
Underlying meaning - I cared for others and was able to endure hardship by supporting my classmate to go to the hospital. - People should support each other.	Underlying meaning - My hard work and assiduous efforts will pay off eventually. - I enjoy spending time with friends and our friendship is genuine.	Underlying meaning	Underlying meaning

What positive personality traits have you identified in these experiences? From those events, what are the overall comments you have on yourself? _____

The worker also needs to help the client develop a checklist on strengths and abilities. As mentioned, these strengths and abilities of the client would be out in the client's Piggy Bank for future exploration in the recovery process.

Intervention tool: Identifying Community Resources

Case background

Mrs. Chan was in her fifties when she was referred to the Integrated Community Centre for Mental Wellness for service. She studied abroad when she was young and worked as a professional after graduation. Later, she got married and became a full-time housewife, taking care of her only son. The marriage of Mrs. Chan was an unhappy one. Soon after she got married, Mrs. Chan suspected that her husband was having an affair. Furthermore, her husband was a gambling addict and had lost all their family savings. Their marital relationship worsened and Mrs. Chan subsequently had depression.

Mrs. Chan had severe depression for more than a decade. She had multiple suicidal attempts, and on many of those occasions, she even tried to kill herself in front of her son who then had to stop his mother from doing so. Over the years, Mrs. Chan had to face financial pressure and marital problems and her mental status fluctuated. Despite these circumstances, she had good compliance to medication.

Several years ago, a number of Mrs. Chan's relatives passed away. She was not able to get over the sadness and had a relapse. The psychiatrist considered that Mrs. Chan needed counselling in addition to her medical treatment and referred her to the Integrated Community Centre for Mental Wellness for service.

Phase IV of Mrs. Chan's recovery

When Mrs. Chan first started counselling, her emotions were still very unstable. She cried every day, suffered from insomnia, and was very forgetful. Whenever she thought of her husband's behaviour she would be overwhelmed by negative emotions. On occasion, Mrs. Chan could not stop crying throughout the counselling session and the session could not continue due to her inconsolable sadness.

Initially, the primary goal of Mrs. Chan was to get a divorce. For her, this seemed to be an ultimate solution to all her troubles. She thought that once she got a divorce, she could be free from feeling hurt by her husband as there would be no more expectations of him. Life would improve, and she could live freely and her sadness would be gone.

The worker then discussed with Mrs. Chan practical steps in processing a divorce and why she did not take any such step previously. On exploration, it seemed that the major barrier for Mrs. Chan in getting a divorce was a fear of financial difficulties. Her husband was the only breadwinner in the family, and her son, who was still studying, relied on her husband for financial support. Another issue was the place of residence. If Mrs. Chan decided to get a divorce, she had to move out from the public housing unit that was under her husband's name and it was difficult for her to find another place to live. After the discussion, Mrs. Chan started to realize that obtaining a divorce was more complicated than she thought. Unlike what she imagined, her grief and troubles would not disappear immediately after the divorce, and that divorce might not be the ultimate solution to all the problems she was facing.

Through the Personal Strengths Assessment form, the worker learned the dreams and aspirations of Mrs. Chan. She longed to return to the time before she was married, the time when she was living abroad and leading a carefree life. In one session, the topic of one's appearance came up and it began to dawn on Mrs. Chan that she still wanted to look pretty in front of her husband and wanted to improve the relationship. The assessment form helped to clarify the thoughts and aspirations of Mrs. Chan.

However, in reality, Mrs. Chan often just stayed at home, feeling gloomy and let her imagination run wild. She indulged herself in the good old times and lacked the energy to go forward. It became a vicious cycle: she was bored because she stayed at home all the time → having nothing to keep her occupied, she recalled the good old times and made comparison with her present situation → increased feeling of sadness → volition decreased further. To break the vicious cycle, the worker tried to engage her in some activities by using the cognitive behaviour therapy (CBT) technique of Activity Ruler. The objective of this technique was to help her identify activities she was interested in that were also relevant to her recovery.

The worker invited Mrs. Chan to complete the Activity Ruler (see Worksheet 04) by listing out ten activities she was interested in and placing two scores to each item according to: (1) the degree of satisfaction the activity brings, and (2) the level of difficulties in doing the activity. The ten activities Mrs. Chan wrote down included exploring nature on her own, hiking with friends, manicures, knitting, cooking, and so on. Both indoor and outdoor activities were listed, and interestingly, outdoor activities were assessed by Mrs. Chan as more difficult to do but giving her more pleasure.

While completing the worksheet, Mrs. Chan mentioned that she felt most nostalgic about her life abroad. She remembered going to the lawn, the park, and the square as she wished, having a cup of coffee, and just having a relaxing time. She longed to return to such a leisurely and comfortable life. She also wanted to meet up with her friends but was taken aback by the high transportation expenses. Similarly, travelling expenses were also a hindrance for her to visit the countryside. Furthermore, gatherings with friends also involved meal charges, and all these created stress for her.

After identifying what Mrs. Chan was struggling with, the worker decided to help her identify community resources available that could help her achieve her goals and take a step forward in the road to recovery.

Concept and purpose of the technique

By helping the client identify and utilize external resources available in the community, strength-based cognitive behaviour therapy (SBCBT) can help him/her achieve his/her goals, facilitate community participation, and encourage personal growth and a more meaningful way of living. The repertoire of resources available in the community can be very broad and can be understood as the external resources of the client. These include public facilities in the neighbourhood such as libraries, sports fields, parks, accessible shopping, and marketplaces; welfare services such as financial assistance and legal aid; a support network of family members and friends; and mental health services.

When exploring community resources with the client, the worker can empower the client by enabling him/her to exercise his/her rights as a citizen, making use of appropriate public services and facilities, and strengthening his/her sense of community. This is also very important for the client to be integrated back into the community. If and when the client gets familiarized with the resources available in the community and learns to use them when needed, he/she would be able to lead a fruitful life independently without the help of the worker.

Operational procedure

The worker realized that the main barrier for Mrs. Chan to achieve her goal of joining outdoor activities was high transportation costs. To address this concern, the worker provided information on the government policy on concessionary fares for people with disabilities. As Mrs. Chan was diagnosed as suffering from mental illness, she would be eligible for the benefit. Once approved, she would just need to pay a minimal flat rate of HK$2 for most public transports in Hong Kong.

Like many people in Hong Kong, initially Mrs. Chan did not feel comfortable about applying for the concessionary fare scheme for fear of the stigma attached to receiving welfare. From her perspective, she did not have physical disability and therefore it was not right for her to receive any financial aid from the government. The worker helped her weigh the pros and cons of getting the concessionary fare. While she might or might not get stigmatized, she would experience less social isolation because the benefits would allow her to use public transport without much cost and would likely enhance her life quality and emotional health. In addition, once she felt better, she could stop receiving the benefit when she resumed work and played a role in contributing back to the community, which she very much wanted to do.

After much consideration, however, Mrs. Chan still had reservations about the application (e.g., the number of supporting documents required and the complexity of the application procedure). In view of the poor relationship she had with her husband, Mrs. Chan feared that her husband would not be cooperative in the application. In response to her worries, the worker checked the relevant application criteria and procedures together with Mrs. Chan. After fact checking, Mrs. Chan was reassured of the relatively simple procedure in the application and the fact that there was no means-testing for the service. Finally, Mrs. Chan's worries were relieved.

After Mrs. Chan successfully applied for the concessional fare, the worker made plans with Mrs. Chan on how to use the benefits in achieving her goal of visiting friends, hiking, and so on. In the process, the worker provided Mrs. Chan with assistance and suggestions to increase her knowledge on public transport and routes she might not be familiar with. The worker also provided information on scenic spots so that Mrs. Chan had the opportunity to gain the freedom that she treasured so much while living abroad.

When Mrs. Chan started to familiarize herself with these community resources, she learned that one of her friends had terminal-stage cancer. Fortunately, Mrs. Chan no longer needed to worry about the transportation costs and was able to visit her friend frequently. She also tried to help her friend in achieving her last wishes. Her friend had died in peace and Mrs. Chan was able to say farewell to her friend without regret. It seemed that this experience also helped her in relieving some of the unresolved issues she had had when someone close to her died.

Outcome

For Mrs. Chan, the concessionary fare benefit enabled her to get in touch with her friends more. She had more opportunities to go out and there was no need for her to face life's challenges and her negative emotions all by herself. Her social life had been expanded and Mrs. Chan spent more time with her friends. This had improved her emotion tremendously. Furthermore, being able to go to places freely also improved her mood and she became happier.

During the time when her friend was dying, she did a lot for her. Although the experience was still a sad one, she felt it was much better than when her family member died. She became more mature in managing death and bereavement.

With the help of the worker, Mrs. Chan made use of a community resource for the first time. This experience made her feel that accessing community resources was not as difficult as she had thought and she became more confident to do it again. She had taken the first step and would be able to move forward without much assistance from others. Lastly, her confidence in accessing external resources also became one of her internal resources.

Reflection

While office-based individual counselling can help the client in clarifying his/her thinking, increases self-understanding and insights, and deals with emotional disturbances, community participation is equally important for a client's well-being. A strong social network and a sense of identity in the community are important elements of psychological well-being. Therefore, one of the critical components in SBCBT is to be able to shift the client's focus from his/her own problem to making social contacts. This is one of the reasons behind identifying and utilizing external resources in the recovery model. For Mrs. Chan, using appropriate community resources not only brought positive changes in emotion, it also facilitated other positive experiences and improvements.

Generally speaking, when helping the client to identify community resources, the worker should pay attention to whether the client is ready to make social contact. Some recovery persons may not be prepared psychologically. In the case of Mrs. Chan, she already had a lot of friends and her social network was not limited. The barriers for Mrs. Chan to develop her social life were her fear of social stigma, financial difficulties, and her lack of knowledge on available resources. If the client is socially withdrawn due to psychological reasons, the worker may need more time to work with his/her psychological barriers before he/she is ready to use community resources.

Conclusion

As the term 'strength-based cognitive behaviour therapy model' conveys, identifying strengths is obviously a major component of the SBCBT model on mental health recovery. The process of identifying internal strengths and external resources itself is therapeutic because clients can identify the past, current, and potential strengths and resources and can begin to visualize how their strengths and resources can be utilized to fulfil the formulated goals in the recovery process. The various exercises presented in this chapter are useful practical strategies and tools that can help a client to identify his/her internal strengths and external resources.

7 Phase V: Setting up tasks, strategies, and plans in achieving the goals

Introduction

In Phase V, the worker assists the client in setting concrete and feasible tasks or action plans to achieve the goals set in Phase IV. A step-by-step approach should be used where long-term goals should be broken down into smaller ones and interim tasks or strategies should be set to facilitate the attainment of the desired outcomes. The Life Goal Formulation Chart in Chapter 5 has captured this goal formulation and planning process. This chapter will introduce how the stated goals can be implemented in the mental health recovery process. An important message that needs to be brought forward here is that, such implementation should be one involving providing our clients with new and successful experiences that promote confidence and commitment to achieving a meaningful life in the mental health recovery process. The worker should not be too pushy nor facilitate the client to set too difficult a task for him/herself because the principle is to build up a sense of competence and to minimize the chance of negative or failed experience. Two cases will be used below to illustrate the application of two strategies: Creating New Experiences and the Behavioural Experiment technique.

Intervention tool: Creating New Experience

The background of Mandy was described in Chapter 3 in this book.

Phase VI of Mandy's recovery

After completing the Personal Strengths Assessment form, Mandy has prioritized her goals in recovery, setting 'improving emotions' as her first priority. Mandy worked as a clerk in a company, and generally speaking, her negative emotions come from her relationship with colleagues. She always felt being discriminated against by her superior and senior colleagues in the arrangement of work assignments. Mandy was highly dissatisfied but afraid to express how she felt. She believed that nothing would change even if she expressed her views. Therefore, it had become a habit for her to bottle up her feelings. As a result, Mandy's emotions were affected, her sleep quality was poor, and she had palpitations.

In fact, Mandy had similar feelings of being prejudiced against in other workplaces as well. She often felt that her superiors and colleagues harbored ill feelings towards her. Indeed, she had quit her previous jobs due to difficulties in her relationship with colleagues. However, similar problems often repeated themselves in other workplaces. The worker suspected that as compared with the likelihood of the client being pinpointed by every colleague she encountered, it was more probable that the problem stemmed from her. In the previous phases, the worker had used the strength-based cognitive behaviour therapy (SBCBT) tool of Situational Self-Analysis exercise and identified that the common thought trap for Mandy was mind reading. Without any evidence, she often concluded that her superiors and colleagues picked on her intentionally. After understanding the concept of thought traps, Mandy started to question the truthfulness of her thoughts. However, all the incidences she recalled happened in the past and there was no way for Mandy to verify whether or not her interpretation of events was biased. Instead of challenging the interpretations she had of the past events, it was hypothesized that similar situations would repeat themselves in a vicious cycle and could affect Mandy's emotions if the problem began with her. Indeed, the worker felt that this biased thinking had served as a major obstacle for Mandy in improving her emotions.

To eliminate Mandy's barriers to achieving her goals, the worker used the technique of Creating New Experiences to encourage her to adopt alternative coping strategies to break the vicious cycle and to increase positive experiences in interpersonal relationships.

Concept and purpose of the technique

When people are in a stressful situation, it is common for them to process it by habitual ways of thinking and behaviour. However, some thought or behavioural patterns may lead to negative outcomes. If the client is not aware of the interplay between maladaptive cognition, emotion, and behaviour, the situation will repeat itself.

Initiating change in one component of this repeated vicious cycle may bring about different outcomes, thus allowing the client to break this dysfunctional cycle. The role of the worker is to encourage the client to make changes, help him/her obtain positive experiences, and subsequently, break away from the habitual response pattern. Once the client has a taste of the positive experience, the worker should highlight the strengths involved and reinforce such changes made by the client.

Operational procedure

The first step is to understand the client's difficulties and the cognitive and behavioural barriers he/she is facing. Second, based on the client's barriers, design practical tasks that are expected to provide positive experiences for him/her. The worker should also encourage the client to work on those tasks, obtain positive experiences, and bring about changes in his/her way of thinking. In the third step, after completing the task, the worker would collaborate with the client to examine and consolidate the new experience, identify internal and external resources, and remind the client constantly to write down these positive experiences and strengths for future reference.

Both techniques, Creating New Experiences and Behaviour Experiment (to be revealed later), aim to open the door for new experiences for the client and change the old and dysfunctional patterns of response. The difference is that Behaviour Experiment is based on the negative thoughts/assumptions the client already has, and through experimentation, challenges the validity of those thoughts; whereas the technique of Creating New Experiences is to create new activities for the client to try and experience. Both techniques ultimately aim at expanding and changing the mindset and the subsequent behaviours of the client.

Case illustration

Before using the Creating New Experiences technique, the worker had explored thoroughly Mandy's experiences about her working relationships with her superiors and colleagues by using the Situational Self-Analysis exercise. Through discussing the Dysfunctional Cycle of Responses, the worker had brainstormed with Mandy alternative ways of responding to similar situations if they were to come up again, and how her emotions, cognitions, and behaviours could be different if she were to think and behave differently (i.e., Functional Cycle of Responses).

At one point, due to an employee shortage, Mandy's superior asked her to take up more duties. Apart from feeling stressed, Mandy also felt she was being unfairly treated. Like before, she believed that her superior was picking on her; and as usual, she just bottled it up without saying anything. She was afraid to express her opinion and thought that even if she did, her views would not be taken seriously and there was nothing she could do to change anything. The worker helped Mandy understand the dysfunctional vicious cycle resulting from her negative thoughts and encouraged her to respond differently by letting her superior realize her heavy workload.

At the beginning, Mandy felt too timid to try. She considered making such a request to her superior too awkward and she was afraid that her superior would reject her request. To encourage Mandy to try, the worker worked with her to consider every possible scenario and to develop a practical action plan. Eventually, the plan Mandy used was to send a message to her superior to request a short meeting when both of them were in the office. With encouragement from the worker, Mandy eventually sent the message, and soon, got a reply from her superior asking her to meet in the superior's office.

Mandy initially thought that her superior would just ignore what she said. On the contrary, her superior listened carefully, showed understanding of her heavy workload, and promised that the arrangement was just temporary as they were going to recruit new staff members. This positive response of her superior was totally beyond Mandy's expectation. Using this as an example of a new experience, the worker pointed out that a change in her habitual ways of responding (i.e., took the initiative to call a meeting with the superior rather than timidly accepting the circumstance as she used to do) could lead to very different outcomes in her life. The worker also helped her draw a Functional Cycle of Responses using the new experience, thus reinforcing the importance of trying something different to break the dysfunctional cycle.

Lastly, the worker helped Mandy to write down this new experience as a reminder. As people tend to be forgetful and it takes time to make changes, recording the new experience can help clients form a deeper impression of the changes. Mandy could then retrieve the written reminder in the future when needed, as a self-reinforcement and reminder.

Outcome

After working on creating the new experience, Mandy started to realize the rigidity and malfunctions of her thoughts and behavioural patterns. The new experience raised her awareness of the thought trap of mind reading. Mandy could also use this new experience as a reminder and the self-debating technique to verify her thoughts with facts. As a next step, Mandy wanted to work on her thought trap of mind reading, which resulted in the suppression of her resentful feelings, to expressing her views and needs more openly.

Another obvious outcome noted was her physical health. Mandy used to feel tightness in the chest when she was emotionally disturbed and she had to take medication to relieve the symptoms. With time, she became dependent on the medication. This new experience not only relieved her worries, the tightness in her chest was gone as well. Creating a new experience not only helped her psychologically, but also physically as well.

The road to recovery requires a lot of courage as one needs to walk out of the comfort zone to try to make changes. But it is more easily said than done. Indeed, continuous support and validation are greatly needed to facilitate the client to make and appreciate incremental changes. However, a client's own motivation is of prime importance. For Mandy, her positive outcome was a result of her willingness to try something different. Her courage and the new experience are all new resources that helped her move on.

Reflection

The most difficult part in using the Creating New Experiences technique is to motivate the client to try something different. Take the case of Mandy as an example: Rationally, Mandy knew it was stressful but fruitless to guess what her superior was thinking, but she could not help it and her fear was real. Under this circumstance, the worker had to examine every detail with her with all possible scenarios such as the best timing — when was a suitable a time (when her boss was not so busy), where should the meeting be held, any person she should avoid when making the contact, and so on.

The worker also needs to go through every small step carefully with the client based on the actual situation. What seems to be an easy move may in fact be a big challenge for the client. As this exercise aims at enhancing success, the worker needs to make careful plans collaboratively with the client because this will give the client the confidence to face the challenge. In the process, it is crucial for the worker to put extra effort into encouraging the client, and work with him/her to imagine every possible scenario so that the client is psychologically prepared.

Even if the outcome is not as good as expected, it is important that the worker still show appreciation of the client's willingness to put in the effort. This reinforces the client to appreciate the efforts, not just the outcomes.

Intervention tool: Behavioural Experiment

Case background

Yana was in her early thirties when she was referred for service. She had been suffering from psychosis with depressive symptoms for more than ten years. Her first onset was triggered by stress at work in her first job. She then stayed at home for several years to avoid the potentially stressful work environment. Due to her family's financial circumstances, Yana had to work again.

Yana was introverted and passive. At work, she was often scolded by her superior. At home, although her family members were good to her, she often felt inferior to her sister. For Yana, her sister's personality was ideal — active, optimistic, and sociable. On the other hand, Yana, being very quiet, had very few friends and felt awkward among her peers.

Yana started receiving service at the Integrated Community Centre for Mental Wellness in 2014. At the time of referral, Yana's mental condition was relatively stable and her psychotic symptom was in remission. However, due to work stress and social anxieties, she would fall into a depressive mood state easily and was very much disturbed by it. Yana blamed all of life's mishaps on her quiet personality, which, she believed, had resulted in her interpersonal problems. She thought that her work performance could be better if it were not for her introverted character. Yana felt that the only way to deal with her situation was to change her personality. If she were similar to her sister, she could make a lot of friends, feel happier, have better work performance, and enjoy work more. Changing her personality became the only goal for Yana.

Phase V of Yana's recovery

The worker noted how Yana tended to attribute all her unhappiness to her personality, to the extreme extent that she believed if she were like her sister, she could definitely enjoy every aspect of her life.

On exploration, the worker found that Yana's self-criticism started in her teens. Yana's younger sister was extroverted, active, sociable, and was praised and loved by family members and friends. Because Yana realized that people generally liked her sister better, she made comparisons and decided that it was her quietness and introverted personality that made her unlikable and unlovable.

Her social experiences reinforced Yana's belief of quiet personality as a negative personality trait. For example, when she had a meal with friends, people sitting on either side of her would start talking to each other. She felt out of place but not able to join the conversation. Being a passive person, she felt like an isolated island in the crowd. A lot of the time, Yana would just lower her head and eat her meal. Another common social situation for Yana was that she was always the one on her own while other people would chat in small groups. These scenarios upset her and she believed that it was due to her undesirable personality.

She felt that she was too quiet and did not know how to strike up a conversation. This was highly uncomfortable for her. Whenever this happened, she would blame herself for being too passive. Yana was certain that she was weird. When she could no longer stand the uncomfortable feelings, she would leave the scene early. These situations were very disturbing to Yana and she blamed and disliked herself even more.

At work, most of her colleagues agreed that Yana's superior was hot-tempered. The supervisor often scolded junior employees in a stern manner, including Yana. But Yana felt that she was being criticized for her poor performance due to her passivity. Whenever she was scolded by her supervisor, she would automatically blame herself. The harsh words from her superior seemed to reinforce her belief that she had performed poorly. She often criticized herself for being careless, lacking detailed planning, and preparing inadequately. However, on exploration, the worker found that Yana had already done a good job. It was just that she lacked confidence. At the beginning of the counselling service, Yana told the worker that due to work stress, she lost her appetite and the quality of her sleep had deteriorated. Although she was still able to go to work, she felt low in energy and could not concentrate.

Initially, Yana thought that changing her personality would be the goal of her recovery. After exploration, the worker noticed her tendency in negative automatic thoughts. After working through the Situational Self-Analysis exercise, Yana gradually understood her typical thought traps such as arbitrary inference, disqualifying the positive, and personalization. She also realized her tendency of attributing everything to having undesirable personality traits. The worker helped Yana realize that what needed to be changed was not her personality, but her way of thinking and behaving. The worker pointed out that to deal with her issues, Yana should accept herself as who she was and recognize the positive side of her introverted personality.

In the process of helping Yana, the worker found that her dysfunctional beliefs/assumptions about personality were very extreme and rigid. The worker then used the Behaviour Experiment technique to work with her belief that being an introvert is undesirable.

Concept and purpose of the technique

Behaviour Experiment is generally used to help a client to challenge his/her unverified beliefs and assumptions, identify cognitive blind spots, and break the dysfunctional beliefs and assumptions. Practically, the worker collaborates with the client to develop a behaviour experiment based on his/her dysfunctional belief or assumption so that the client is able to test the validity of the belief or assumption. After completing the experiment, the worker helps the client to review the experience and to analyze if the assumption/belief is indeed true fact.

The four steps in a Behaviour Experiment are:

1 Identify beliefs: observe and analyze the thinking pattern of the client, identify the rigid and dysfunctional belief or assumption.
2 Set tasks: assist the client in designing a corresponding and feasible experiment to verify if his/her belief is true and rational.
3 Experiment: encourage the client to put the proposed experiment into action.
4 Review and analysis: after completing the experiment, review the experience and the outcome with the client, compare the results with the original belief, and examine the differences.

Case illustration

IDENTIFY BELIEFS OR ASSUMPTIONS

When the worker helped Yana to identify her internal strengths and resources, Yana was able to mention a number of positive characteristics. However, she later denied them completely when the worker wrote them down. She insisted that she had no positive characteristics whatsoever and strongly believed that being introverted was no good.

With the view of exploring the perceptions with Yana, the worker then discussed with Yana the pros and cons of different personality traits. During the exploration, Yana expressed that at times, she felt that talkative people could also be irritating. People who were good talkers might not have advantages in all occasions. Yana also mentioned a friend of hers who was also rather quiet. On further probing, Yana mentioned she felt comfortable relating with this friend. Notwithstanding this, she still adamantly believed that her own quiet character was a negative trait for her.

Yana was highly irrational concerning her own personality. The deep-rooted rigid belief had greatly affected her negative emotions and behaviours.

SET TASKS

To work with the belief that being an introvert is a negative personality trait, the worker used two tasks with Yana. First, the worker invited Yana to take note of how introverted people related with others, whether it differed from hers, and whether these people's emotion was affected by their interpersonal relationships. Second, the worker invited Yana to ask her "quiet" friends directly about their views on such personality and to compare it with her own thinking, to determine whether these friends also felt bad about being an introvert or whether they would have other views.

EXPERIMENT

When Yana met her introverted friends again, she did the following: (1) observed how they related with others, and (2) asked their views on introverted personality.

After doing the tasks, Yana noticed that, in fact, her introverted friends seemed to be quite at ease in social situations, which was very different from her uncomfortable feelings. For these friends, the personality trait was not a barrier in interpersonal relationships. As their friend herself, Yana's own experience also verified that their relationship was not affected by her quiet personality.

When Yana asked these friends their views on introverted personality, they did not view being an introvert as problematic or undesirable. Furthermore, they thought that this was a positive personality trait in interpersonal relationships. Yana realized that other people's views were quite different from hers.

REVIEW AND ANALYSIS

Obviously, both Behaviour Experiments have clearly refuted her belief or assumption of being an introvert is an undesirable personality trait (Table 7.1). Because Yana had close relationships with the friends on whom she did the experiment, she was confident that the answers were genuine. Responses from her close friends naturally carried more weight than that of the worker and had effectively challenged her rigid belief.

Outcome

Behaviour Experiment is a technique where the client has to learn by experience. It is generally more powerful than getting the information from the worker and is more effective in challenging the client's rigid mindset. Although Yana did not have a dramatic shift in her perception on personality traits, she no longer could convince herself that being an introvert is undesirable. She became less critical of herself and from her own experience, she knew that her introverted friends did not make her feel uncomfortable at all.

Table 7.1 Behaviour Experiment worksheet of Yana

Behaviour Experiment worksheet

1   What is the psychological blind spot that needs to be challenged?

Introverted and quiet personality is not desirable.

2   Describe the issue precisely in concrete terms:

   a   What does 'introverted and quiet personality' mean?

      Examples: Lack of conversation topics in social situations.

               Being passive in social situations.

   b   How would someone with 'good personality' behave?

      Examples: Extroverted and active like my sister.

               Able to strike up a conversation with friends easily and rich in conversation topics.

3   Details of the behaviour experiment (feasible and likely to have positive results):

   a   Observe friends who are introverted on how they relate with others, compare it with your own situation and check if their emotions are affected by interpersonal relationships.

   b   Ask introverted friends on their views of their own personality to check if they also see being introverted undesirable.

4   Review of the experience (Any difference from your previous thoughts/understanding? What are the differences? What did you learn from it?)

I noticed that my introverted friends were at ease in interpersonal relationships. They did not feel uncomfortable or troubled by their personality. And being an introvert was not a barrier in their interpersonal relationships. It was also comfortable for me to relate with these introverted friends.

My friends did not consider their introverted personality undesirable. On the contrary, they felt that their personality made people feel comfortable when relating to them. I realized that other people might have completely different views from me and that being an introvert was not as bad as I thought.

Initially, it was difficult for Yana to identify and acknowledge her internal strengths. After the Behaviour Experiment, Yana became more willing to accept her own strengths and ready to make use of them. The results of the Behaviour Experiment enabled Yana to accept herself more and her negative emotions arising from self-negation were reduced. Yana became more at ease in social situations and her work performance greatly improved.

From self-blaming and self-criticism, Yana now adopted a more objective and less rigid attitude. At work, she learned to differentiate what were her responsibilities and what were not. She started to notice that her superior's behaviour was the same to everyone and she was not the only one being scolded. She accepted that stern words from her boss were not due to her personal inadequacy, it was just his bad temper.

Before, Yana often compared herself with her sister. Her sister was perfect while she was inadequate. With a broadened mindset, she realized that in reality, her sister was not as perfect as she imagined and had her own issues, too. She accepted herself more and became more objective in making judgments about personality.

In social gatherings, Yana became much more relaxed. Though she remained a quiet member in the group, this did not upset her. Her previous uncomfortable feelings about not being able to strike a conversation had lessened. From feeling somewhat weird, Yana began to feel she was just normal and ordinary. Yana had taken a big step in the road to recovery.

Reflection

The critical component in Behaviour Experiment is designing appropriate experiments. In the case of Yana, it was easy for the worker to identify her dysfunctional beliefs/assumptions but it took quite some time to work out the design of the experiment. Therefore, in implementing this tool, the worker has to be innovative and design the experiment based on the situation of the individual client.

Whether the client feels safe or competent is also important consideration in designing the experiment. An experiment should be feasible and the circumstances safe enough to motivate the client to try. In the case of Yana, if the individuals she was asked to observe or talk to were her colleagues or superiors instead of friends, Yana would definitely be unwilling to do so. Even if she finally did conduct the experiment with her colleagues or boss, the degree of the impact would be much less. Furthermore, if the content of the experiment goes beyond the capacity of the client, it is also more difficult for the client to take action. Therefore, in designing the experiment, the worker needs to take into account the sense of security and the ability of the client and make plans appropriately and accordingly.

Lastly, changes in a client's beliefs and assumptions are best achieved by new experiences because the client has gone through the process to achieve a new perspective and outlook about certain issues, oneself, and/or others. In the process, it is important to conduct debriefing close to the time of the experience to consolidate what the client has learned about the issue, oneself, and/or others.

Conclusion

Mental health recovery is a personal journey and the recovering person must go through the experiences to arrive at a new understanding of him/herself and others, and to achieve a new meaning in life for him/herself. The worker's roles are to facilitate and support the recovering person to achieve his/her stated goals. Rather than focusing on past experiences, clients must create new experiences, facilitated by the worker, so that they can see and experience new possibilities in life. It is also hoped that the accumulation of new experiences will lead to the development of a liberated self in the individual.

8 Phase VI: Identifying individual or environmental barriers to achieving goals

Introduction

During the recovery process, the recovering person is bound to face obstacles that impede his/her goal attainment. These obstacles can come from internal and external sources. Internally, the client's lack of awareness of his/her own strengths, dysfunctional patterns of response, and rigid beliefs and assumptions can affect his/her understanding of and confidence in achieving his/her goals. Externally, the limitations present in the environment (e.g., availability of resources and lack of willingness of the system to change and be more responsive to the needs of the client) can also affect whether and how much the client can achieve his/her goals. In this chapter, we describe how the worker can help the client to identify and develop strategies to deal with the internal factors that pose difficulties and barriers in completing a task or implementing a strategy. We use the case of Mrs. Ko to illustrate how to use the 5-Strategies and Costs and Benefits Analysis to facilitate clients to overcome barriers in achieving their recovery goals.

Intervention tool: The 5-Strategies

Case background

The background of Mrs. Ko was described in Chapter 3 of this book.

Phase V of Mrs. Ko's recovery

In Chapter 3, we mentioned that Mrs. Ko was highly motivated to change from the very beginning because she loved her children and did not want them to be affected by her negative emotions. Mrs. Ko was concerned about the parent–child relationship and at the same time, she wanted to do something about her depression. Despite her good intentions, Mrs. Ko could not control her negative emotions, which often ended up in her having temper outbursts. During these episodes, Mrs. Ko would scold and use corporal punishment on her son. Rationally, she realized that this would seriously affect the parent–child relationship and was not good for her emotional health. With this in mind, the goals for recovery for Mrs. Ko were: (1) better emotional management, and (2) improvement in parenting skills.

After Mrs. Ko set the goals, the worker started to collaborate with Mrs. Ko on formulating feasible strategies and setting tasks in achieving those goals. Regarding the goal of improving her parenting skills, the worker helped Mrs. Ko to examine methods that had been used so far and to identify skills that had been successful. These skills were indeed Mrs. Ko's internal resources, and they included praising the child, matching learning goals with the child's ability, treasuring the time spent with the child, and so on. The worker encouraged Mrs. Ko to continue using these internal resources to improve her parenting skills and to strengthen the parent–child relationship. Role plays were also used to help Mrs. Ko learn how to communicate with the child effectively.

With regard to the goal of emotion management, however, although Mrs. Ko had become aware of her thought trap of catastrophizing as well as her behavioural responses of scolding and spanking her child, she had not been able to effectively handle these issues when parenting her children. Her dysfunctional pattern of responses appeared to be strongly spontaneous and she had become more and more frustrated in failing to find effective ways of overcoming her obstacles to achieving the goal of better emotion management. To address this obstacle and to build a sense of success, the cognitive behaviour therapy (CBT) technique of 5-Strategies was used to help her break this dysfunctional cycle by dealing with her catastrophizing style of thinking and building up her emotional management skills.

Concept and purpose of the technique

The 5-Strategies is a strategic planning tool, targeting the dysfunctional pattern of automatic responses. The purpose is to prevent the client from falling into his/her pattern, which then leads to the occurrence and/or escalation of the negative automatic emotional and behavioural responses of the client. Before using the 5-Strategies, the client must have a thorough understanding of the association between thoughts and emotions and should obtain sufficient insight into his/her own dysfunctional thought traps. This understanding of the dysfunctional interaction between thoughts, emotions, and behaviours is a prerequisite to change.

The five strategies used in this technique refer to: (1) be alert of the physiological warning signals; (2) stop negative thoughts; (3) self-disputing questions; (4) distraction; and (5) positive self-statements. The worker helps the client identify certain situations/events that frequently arouse his/her negative emotions and behavioural responses, and assists the client in developing tactics according to the 5-Strategies. The 5-Strategies are tailor-made for the individual client, and the worker should encourage the client to practice the strategies as much as he/she can. With practice, the client gains more confidence in using the strategies and becomes able to change the pattern of his/her dysfunctional responses. In a nutshell, the ultimate objectives of the 5-Strategies are to break the dysfunctional cycle of responses and to build up the strength (i.e., coping ability) and successful experience of the client to resolve his/her obstacles/barriers in the recovery process.

Operational procedure

The 5-Strategies refers to:

BE ALERT OF THE PHYSIOLOGICAL WARNING SIGNALS

The worker should raise the awareness of the client on his/her physiological responses to negative life events and the associated emotions. For example, a faster heartbeat and feeling hot in the face are likely to be associated with anger, while anxiety may be linked to sweating, muscle tension, and so on. It is assumed that physiological responses are natural and autonomous responses people exhibit promptly when facing events in life, and the quicker one can sense those responses, the faster it is for the person to become aware of his/her possible negative emotions, cognitions, and behaviours. In short, these physiological signs are warning signals for an individual to do something about his/her internal states and external events.

STOP NEGATIVE THOUGHTS (I.E., THOUGHT STOPPING TECHNIQUE)

The purpose of stopping the negative thoughts is to give your brain a break in times of confusion. This allows time to prevent oneself from falling into the thought traps and the negative spiral of unending negative thoughts and emotions.

The client can use either a behavioural or verbal reminder to stop negative thoughts. Examples of behavioural reminders include taking deep breaths, drinking a glass of water, and muscle relaxation exercises; verbal reminders can be a short phrase that helps the person to stop negatively thinking right away. Examples include:

Wait a minute, this is not as bad as I imagine!
Stop and think, don't go into a dead end!
Don't think about it anymore!
Stop! Don't be so pessimistic!

SELF-DISPUTING QUESTIONS

Using self-disputing questions facilitates the client to adopt a different perspective in understanding the event/situation. There are two directions in developing a self-disputing question; one direction focuses on developing questions that challenge the client's negative thinking style (i.e., thought trap), and the other direction centers on the contents of the negative thoughts.

The following examples are questions used in challenging the negative thinking style (i.e., thought trap):

Are there other alternative ways of thinking apart from this negative one (i.e., arbitrary inference)?
Are things as bad as I thought (i.e., catastrophic thought)?
Is my judgment based on emotion or rational reasoning (i.e., emotion reasoning)?
Don't others have to take responsibility too (i.e., assumption of responsibility)?

These questions can help to remind the client to examine and challenge his/her thinking style so that he/she can stop engaging further in the negative thoughts.

Examples of questions challenging the negative automatic thought contents are:

When you notice a client of yours feeling very stressful (i.e., to the point of having mental health problems) but continuing to agree to do things for others for fear of not being loved, a self-disputing question for the client would be, 'If I am in poor health condition or feeling stressful all the time, am I able to love and enjoy the love from others?'
Another example is a father who loves his teenage daughter so much so that he becomes overly protective of every little thing she does, which leads to constant arguing and a strained relationship. A good self-disputing question would be, 'Am I loving her or am I losing her by doing what I am doing?'

When helping the client to develop a self-disputing question, it is important for the worker to be aware that the question has to be collaboratively created and that the client has to fully endorse the question. This is necessary for the client to build up confidence in using the strategies because he/she is the one who will have to use the question on a day-to-day basis in the future.

DISTRACTION

When the client is aware of having negative thoughts, he/she can try to shift his/her attention to other irrelevant things. The rationale for using this strategy is to give the client's mind a break from the issue, preventing him/her from indulging in negative thoughts. When refreshed, the person is more ready to deal with the emotions and the issue at hand.

The worker should help the client determine an effective means of distraction, such as going for a walk, taking a shower, listening to music, or watching television. It is important for the worker to facilitate the client to generate a list of possible distraction activities by asking the client about his/her likes and dislikes, interests, what he/she used to enjoy, and so on. Once the list is developed, the worker can help the client rate the effectiveness of each proposed activity in distracting oneself from the negative thoughts.

POSITIVE SELF-STATEMENTS

Positive self-statements refers to personal mottos and words of encouragement that a client can say to him/herself in order to counteract the demoralizing negative thoughts that are running the person down. For example, a client of ours who had vacillating and indecisive thinking style had difficulty making decisions in life, and often felt miserable for missing many chances in life. One motto that we came up with was 'just do it', and we gave him a picture of a popular sports shoe company with a 'tick' to remind him of the motto. The positive self-statement can be put on a card that can be displayed prominently or carried with the client at all times. When the client becomes aware of his/her negative thoughts, he/she can read and contemplate what is written on the smart card and ease his/her emotions and negative thoughts.

Worksheet 05 is designed for the worker to work through the 5-Strategies with the client. The worker can explain each step of the 5-Strategies to the client and explore what internal resources the client can use to put those strategies in daily practice.

In the worksheet, the client is invited to write down one incident that he/she finds emotionally disturbing. The worker then helps the client to identify the associating negative thinking or thought traps. Then, the client is encouraged to record in the worksheet the tactics that he/she can think of under the 5-Strategies. There are a few tips to remember. First, encourage the client to generate as many tactics as he/she can possibly think of. Second, if the client has difficulty generating the tactics, use more promptings and/or even provide suggestions so that the client can later choose the ones that suits him/her. Third, ask the client to rate from 1 to 10 the effectiveness of each proposed tactic and then choose the one he/she wants to try first. Fourth, review the tactics that have been tried and make modifications.

Case illustration

Take the case of Mrs. Ko as an example. As soon as Mrs. Ko saw the examination results of her son, she started to worry about his next examination. Using the Situational Self-Analysis exercise, Mrs. Ko was made aware of the negative thinking behind these worries. She was worried that her son might be inflated with too much ego and became lax in his studies. And then, this might result in a big setback in her son's next examination. Eventually, the deterioration in academic performance would affect his future studies and no school would be willing to enrol him. Through the exercise, Mrs. Ko realized that her thought trap was catastrophizing.

As Mrs. Ko's motivation had increased and her awareness of the catastrophic thought trap had been raised, the worker started to help her develop the 5-Strategies to break her dysfunctional cycle. When going through the exercise, Mrs. Ko became particularly aware of her physiological warning signals. She realized that whenever she felt that her son was having academic problems, she became very stressed and would have a headache (i.e., awareness of physiological warning signals). Then, she would start to experience emotional disturbances. The strategy she devised was to walk away, wash her face, and drink a glass of water (i.e., distraction).

For self-disputing questions, Mrs. Ko constructed, 'Am I pushing my son and myself too hard?', 'Is what I am doing helpful to him and me?', and 'Am I blowing things out of proportion?'. These self-disputing questions were able to calm her down and gave her a different perspective in understanding her son's situation. When composed, she was able to reassure herself that her son was not a sloppy person and he was just happy with the good examination results. Moreover, there was no evidence to show that his ego was excessively inflated because of the success. This technique was able to help Mrs. Ko from falling into the thought traps of arbitrary inference and catastrophizing.

Lastly, Mrs. Ko came up with a positive self-statement to give encouragement to herself. On the smart card, she wrote: 'As long as my son and I have tried our best, whether he can meet the target or make improvement is secondary. There is no need to meet the target each time.' This serves to remind her that for both herself and her son, it is good enough to have tried (Table 8.1).

Outcome

The goals of recovery for Mrs. Ko were to improve her emotional management skills and parenting skills. The 5-Strategies technique provided her a structured action plan for her to manage her emotions. Once her emotional health had improved, it became easier for her to use the parenting skills she already had acquired to nurture the parent–child relationship. Mrs. Ko used to lose her temper easily and would scold or use physical punishment on her child. This had an adverse impact on her parent–child relationship, which Mrs. Ko wanted to get diminish. After she learned the 5-Strategies technique, she could detect her negative thoughts, adjust her negative emotions, and discipline her child in a more appropriate manner.

Mrs. Ko showed obvious improvements during this phase. She was able to identify her negative automatic thoughts accurately and apply the 5-Strategies technique to manage her emotions. Situations where Mrs. Ko resorted to scolding and hitting her son had greatly reduced. Her son was also more willing to communicate with Mrs. Ko and their relationship became closer.

Table 8.1 Mrs. Ko's worksheet on the 5-Strategies

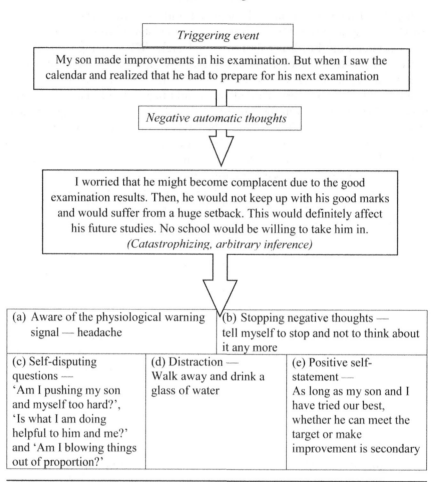

The 5-Strategies

Triggering event
My son made improvements in his examination. But when I saw the calendar and realized that he had to prepare for his next examination

Negative automatic thoughts
I worried that he might become complacent due to the good examination results. Then, he would not keep up with his good marks and would suffer from a huge setback. This would definitely affect his future studies. No school would be willing to take him in. *(Catastrophizing, arbitrary inference)*

(a) Aware of the physiological warning signal — headache		(b) Stopping negative thoughts — tell myself to stop and not to think about it any more	
(c) Self-disputing questions — 'Am I pushing my son and myself too hard?', 'Is what I am doing helpful to him and me?' and 'Am I blowing things out of proportion?'	(d) Distraction — Walk away and drink a glass of water	(e) Positive self-statement — As long as my son and I have tried our best, whether he can meet the target or make improvement is secondary	

The worker affirmed and praised Mrs. Ko's positive changes to reinforce her continuous efforts.

Reflection

The 5-Strategies provide structured steps for a client to develop new and adaptive coping responses (i.e., strengths) to handle life difficulties. These steps are easy for clients to follow. The clients can use the technique independently without the help of the worker. For the case of Mrs. Ko, before she learned the 5-Strategies, she already knew she should leave the scene to drink a glass of water or wash her face to calm herself down. The worker highlighted these as her internal resources and strengths and appreciated her ability in exercising emotional management skills. The recognition and affirmation could raise her sense of competence and increase her confidence in using the technique.

The effect of using strength-based cognitive behaviour therapy (SBCBT) tools may not be the same for clients with different temperament and personality profiles. Mrs. Ko had high cognitive function and was quick to grasp the principles of the various techniques. She was also a highly reflective person. Therefore, it was easy for her to learn and apply the skills. She was also an eager learner and receptive to comments. SBCBT on mental health recovery focuses on exploring the clients' internal and external resources and identifying positive changes. To build up the confidence of Mrs. Ko, in the counselling process, the worker often gave immediate positive feedback on her abilities and the improvements she had made. Mrs. Ko was not used to hearing praise in her daily life and the positive comments from the worker reassured Mrs. Ko of her strengths and reinforced her efforts to make changes.

Some clients may find it hard to break the long-standing habit of falling into their automatic thought traps and have difficulties using the self-debating technique. The worker has to demonstrate in the counselling process how to practically apply this technique. The worker should also give encouragement and provide opportunities for the client to practice. With practice, the client is given the opportunity to explore alternative perspectives to his/her automatic thoughts and get prepared to apply the skills in real-life situations.

Intervention tool: Costs and Benefits Analysis

Case background

The case of Mrs. Ko will be used in this section as well. As described in the previous sections, the goals in recovery for Mrs. Ko were to improve her emotional management skills and parenting skills. Through the Situational Self-Analysis exercise, Mrs. Ko identified the thought trap that triggered her negative emotion was catastrophizing. Behaviourally, Mrs. Ko responded to the emotional trigger by scolding and hitting her child. To achieve the goal of emotional management, Mrs. Ko used the 5-Strategies to avoid falling into her thought trap and to regulate her negative emotions. She also put the positive parenting skills she already knew into use and learned effective communication skills through role play.

After a number of sessions with Mrs. Ko, the worker noticed that she repeatedly mentioned 'my son could not meet the target', 'he could not meet my expectation' — as if in her mind, there was an unbreakable rule and belief that 'we have to meet certain set targets in life'. On exploration, the worker started to understand further the background of Mrs. Ko.

Mrs. Ko lost both her parents when she was young. Her social support network was weak and she had to face life's challenges on her own. She was independent and capable and worked hard to meet every target she set for herself. This also gradually became her personal belief system and rules for life. However, the rules were rigid and she demanded both herself and her son to meet targets without allowing any leeway. This rigidity resulted in emotional disturbances and a barrier for her to achieve her stated goal of emotion management. Therefore, the worker decided to help her identify this barrier, raised her awareness towards her dysfunctional beliefs and assumptions, and facilitated her using the Costs and Benefits Analysis to overcome the barrier.

Concept and purpose of the technique

'Dysfunctional rules' is a collective term that denotes attitudes, beliefs, rules, and values held by an individual. These rules are translated into everyday life expectations and views of an individual towards him/herself and others. It is a standard with which one assesses oneself and others, and is formed by an accumulation of life experiences. For example, someone may hold the rule that 'responsible parents must make sure that their children can receive the best education. If they cannot do it, they are not good parents'. In itself, there is no absolute right or wrong to this rule (i.e., to most rules we have in life), and in some ways, it motivates the parents to try hard to ensure that their children can receive good education. However, if the family is having financial difficulties and the parents still insist on paying the private school tuition fee for their children, they may end up feeling very stressful, frustrated, and even in debt. It is the rigidity and a lack of flexibility that make the rules dysfunctional.

The purpose of Costs and Benefits Analysis is to help a client identify his/her own dysfunctional rules; weigh the costs and benefits of upholding the rule; review whether the rule has become too rigid; examine the nature of the dysfunction; and determine what impacts the rule has on the emotional, interpersonal, and other aspects of a person's life. Through the exercise, the client can become more flexible in applying his/her rules in life.

When the client can realize the negative impacts of his/her dysfunctional rules and is ready to make changes, the worker helps the client to understand that these dysfunctional rules are, in fact, constructed by him/herself to guide his/her thinking and actions, and it is up to oneself to take the initiative to change. The worker can then explore with the client how to relax the dysfunctional rules, making the rules more flexible, adaptable, and more effective.

Operational procedure

In each session in the recovery process, the worker should be highly sensitive to any mention of dysfunctional rules subtly expressed by the client. Where appropriate, the worker should start raising the client's awareness towards these dysfunctional rules and to engage him/her in the Costs and Benefits Analysis. Steps are as follows:

1　Invite the client to write down the dysfunctional rules identified.
2　Invite the client to put a score on the extent to which he/she believes in the identified rule, 1 being the least certain and 5 the most certain.
3　List the advantages and disadvantages of the dysfunctional rule and highlight the impacts it has on the person and other people.
4　Invite the client to rank the importance of each item in the list of advantages and disadvantages with a maximum score of 100. In other words, from 0–100, how much does the client think a particular item has clearly brought out the advantage or disadvantage of holding the identified rule?
5　Add the total scores in the list of advantages and disadvantages.
6　Invite the client to compare the table and analyze the results with the worker. Whether the total score in the disadvantage list is greater or smaller than the score in the advantage list, there are many hints in the table that the worker can choose to discuss with the client to help him/her examine the benefits and losses in holding onto the dysfunctional rules. This exercise also helps to enhance the motivation of the client to relax his/her rules in life.
7　Ask the client to modify the identified rule by rewriting the rule (i.e., change the wording so that it becomes less rigid to the client).
8　Write down the modified dysfunctional rule and assign a new score to it.
9　Examine the advantages and disadvantages the modified rule brings to the client.
10　Facilitate the client to develop behavioural plans to act out the revised rule.

Lastly, the worker provides the client with a memo containing 'Five Slogans to Changing Dysfunctional Rules'. The worker then invites the client to select one slogan that best serves as a reminder for the client to keep relaxing his/her rules.

Case illustration

In terms of parent–child relationship, Mrs. Ko often told the worker that she became irritated and angry if her son could not meet the set 'targets'. In her view, if a person could not meet a target, he/she would be considered a failure. This was also what she expected from her son, that is, he had to complete each learning objective in earnest. Obviously, Mrs. Ko's dysfunctional rule was, 'One must meet one's objectives, if not, one is a failure'. When the worker pointed this out, Mrs. Ko admitted that this was indeed her belief behind everything she did. She set one objective after another and urged herself to accomplish them. Mrs. Ko had put a lot of effort and time into reaching the objectives she set for herself despite the fact that she experienced tremendous pressure. However, she believed that this was the price she had to pay to reach the targets. Thus, she expected the same from her son. The worker therefore invited Mrs. Ko to conduct the Costs and Benefits Analysis exercise (Table 8.2).

Mrs. Ko rated the rule on 'One must meet one's objectives, if not, one is a failure,' a score of 5 in the scale of certainty, meaning that she absolutely believed in this rule.

According to Mrs. Ko, the benefits this rule brought were: (1) gave her and others motivation in life, (2) enabled her to make the best use of time and life, (3) helped her in achieving her objectives, and (4) set a good model for others, including her son. Mrs. Ko also listed the undesirable consequences of her belief: (1) gave herself and others a lot of mental stress and anxiety, (2) an enormous amount of time was needed to learn different things in order to meet objectives, (3) poor quality of sleep, and (4) spent a lot of money to learn new things that might not be useful. After Mrs. Ko listed all the advantages and disadvantages, the worker invited her to score each item and to calculate the total scores.

Table 8.2 Costs and Benefits Analysis worksheet of Mrs. Ko

Costs and benefits analysis

1 Personal rules
I must meet targets I set for myself.
Scale of certainty
certain..................absolutely certain
   1   2   3   4   5

Benefits/pros	score	Disadvantages/cons	score
1 As a motivator in life	80	1 Exerting huge mental stress, makes me and others very anxious and uptight	95
2 Not to waste lifetime	50	2 Wasting most of my time to achieve objectives	65
3 Helpful in achieving my objectives	70	3 Poor sleep quality	65
4 Set as a good model for others	60	4 Wasting money	60
Total **260**		**Total** **285**	

2 Modified/relaxed rules
It is okay not to reach the target immediately as long as I have already tried my best.
Scale of certainty
certain..................absolutely certain
   1   2   3   4   5

Benefits/pros	score	Disadvantages/cons	score
1 Can reduce mental stress for myself and son	90	2 Will not achieve the target as quickly as planned	70

Although Mrs. Ko found that she scored higher in the total scores in the list of disadvantages than the advantages, she did not seem to see the need to modify the rule initially. On the other hand, she believed the slightly higher score in the list of disadvantage echoed her belief in 'no pain, no gain'. To help Mrs. Ko clearly see the disadvantages of the rule, particularly in terms of the parent–child relationship about which she was very much concerned, the worker facilitated her to examine how her dysfunctional rule had affected her mental health, sleep quality, and parent–child relationship. In the process, the worker asked Mrs. Ko to choose, hypothetically, from one of the following, to have a good parent–child relationship and see her son grow up happily, or to have a son who excels in school but feels very stressed and unhappy. Mrs. Ko thought for a moment and then realized that all she really wanted was to see her son happy in life, and that there were many ways to happiness, including excelling in studies.

With this realization, Mrs. Ko decided to rewrite her rule, 'It is okay to allow oneself leeway in trying to reach the target. It may also mean a delay in reaching the goal'. After Mrs. Ko revised the rule, the worker invited her to write down the extent of her certainty of the new rule as well as the benefits and disadvantages. The most obvious benefit of the new rule for Mrs. Ko was that it could lessen her and her son's mental stresses and might improve their parent–child relationship. The worker then asked Mrs. Ko to think of a few concrete examples where she could become a little less pushy towards her son and encouraged her to try to do so in real life.

Outcome

After rewriting the rule, Mrs. Ko used it in parallel with the 5-Strategies and wrote the new rule on her smart card. When she recognized she was having a physical response (headache) while disciplining her child, she would calm herself down and distract herself by leaving the spot for a while to wash her face or drink a glass of water. She also used the smart card to remind herself that as long as she and her son have tried their best, it was okay even if the target could not be reached. As a result, the stress from disciplining her son was significantly reduced and the conflicts between them had lessened. After adjusting her expectations, Mrs. Ko had more control in pushing her son to do revisions. With less tension between them, she was able to observe the efforts and the improvements made by her son as well. She also put into practice the parenting skills and communication skills she had learned. She spent time having fun with her son and took him out to play just like what her mother did when she was a child. The parent–child relationship had improved significantly. Ironically, her son's interest in learning increased and he was able to take the initiative to share his feelings with Mrs. Ko and helped with the household chores.

Paradoxically, when Mrs. Ko started to lessen her insistence to meet targets she placed onto herself and her son, then she was able to achieve the objectives of emotional management and improvement in parent–child relationships. This was a big step in her road to recovery. After Mrs. Ko overcame the barriers resulting from her dysfunctional rules, the worker also observed other positive changes in Mrs. Ko. For example, she learned how to adjust her expectations towards her son, was able to accept his limitations, was willing to spend time and had more patience in communicating with him, and praised and gave him recognition and tried to explore his strengths. Throughout the process, the worker tried to validate Mrs. Ko's gains and gave her recognition and praise when these positive changes were noted. However, as Mrs. Ko seldom received this positive recognition and praise, she was a bit reluctant to accept compliments when the worker showed appreciation. But gradually, she recognized her own changes and responded to the worker's praise with a happy smile and by nodding her head in self-approval.

The five slogans to relaxing one's dysfunctional rules

The following are five slogans that serve as reminders for oneself to relax and rewrite one's dysfunctional rules.

Slogan One: 'Relax a little and gain more'

The reality does not often match our expectations, and it is futile to insist and remain steadfast in one's position. Furthermore, unrealized or unfinished high expectations often make oneself and the people around you unhappy and dissatisfied. Remember, 'step back and think from a broader perspective', and you can also ask yourself: 'what impacts does my insistence have on me and others?'.

Slogan Two: 'Don't hold onto the old rule, make constant refinement'

Some rules come from deep-rooted cultural beliefs and values. However, over time, some of these cultural values and beliefs become too rigid and dated and are inappropriate in modern times. If we still insist on upholding these traditional values in real life, it can only make you and others around you feel unhappy.

Slogan Three: 'Treat yourself well and lighten up your responsibility'

Some people consider certain rules their ultimate standards and responsibilities. If they cannot meet those standards or fulfil those responsibilities, they are a total failure. This attitude brings about a lot of stress and is very exhausting to the person. It would also be very frustrating if the person feels he/she is not up to par to the standards. Give yourself a break.

Slogan Four: 'Treat others well and discard your biases'

At times, we will unintentionally demand others to comply with our values or judgments and expect them to do what we think is right. When people do things differently, we are unhappy and are not satisfied with their behaviours. This affects our interpersonal relationship tremendously. Give others a break.

Slogan Five: 'We have the freedom to make and modify rules'

Rules are self-made and you have no obligation to follow them through. Besides, these rules are not unbreakable. If we are willing to 'choose' another perspective and allow the rules to relax a bit, it would be easier both on ourselves and people around us. Why not give it a try? You can choose to change your rules.

Reflection

Dysfunctional rules held by people are generally not expressed directly. The worker should learn to listen carefully and pay attention to the dysfunctional thoughts and behavioural responses made by the client. Very often, certain common themes will stand out from the pattern of responses. For instance, when a client seems to be constantly engaging in conflicts with her husband, particularly, in relation to how they should raise their child (i.e., a theme), it is possible that she may have a certain rule or belief about the proper role of a husband in raising a child (e.g., 'husband should always set good example for his child').

Another easy technique in tapping the rule of a client is to ask certain follow-up questions. For example, if a client expresses, 'I should not have sought help', the worker can probe further by asking, 'If you ask for help, what does that mean about you?' (e.g. I am useless). Also, when exploring thought traps, the worker can also make a suggestion on the first part of the sentence and then guide the client to complete the full statement, 'If you do … [this], what does that reflect on you?'.

In Mrs. Ko's case, during the interview, the worker noticed that she frequently mentioned her expectations on her son's obedience and meeting standards; and she also expected herself to 'meet standards'. The worker followed up on this direction and asked, 'What does it mean if standards are not met?' Through this exploration, the worker could then identify the dysfunctional rule of Mrs. Ko: 'A person is a failure if he/she cannot meet the standard'.

It is also important for the worker to adopt an open, accepting, and nonjudgmental attitude, as well as encourage an environment of self-determination for the client. The worker should stress that there is no right or wrong in one's rules or beliefs. In fact, the worker should point out that everyone needs to rely on some rules to guide his/her behaviour when making a judgment. Problems arise only when some of these rules are unreasonable and/or rigid. The important point is to relax the rules so that they can become flexible in applying to oneself and others. In doing so, the client can avoid falling into the trap of self-criticism where one cannot recognize and appreciate one's own strengths.

When modifying the rules, a client's self-determination should always be respected. The worker should respect the client's preferences in the use of terms and phrases in rewriting the rules and whether he/she decides to replace the old rule with the modified one.

Conclusion

Although SBCBT and the recovery approach in general devote much energy in identifying and developing strengths and resources of a client, it is critical for the client and worker to make efforts to identify and find ways of overcoming the barriers to goal attainment in the client's recovery process as well. Certain obstacles can seriously stifle the positive effects of goal attainment in the recovery process and demoralize the individual from continuing to work towards attaining the stated goals. In this chapter, two conventional CBT strategies, the 5-Strategies and Cost and Benefits Analysis, have been described in detail for tackling some of the internal psychological barriers that influence the client's progress in recovery.

9 Phase VII: Engaging in continuous review and feedback

Introduction

Phase VII is the final phase of the strength-based cognitive behaviour therapy (SBCBT) model on mental health recovery. It focuses on the issues and importance of conducting continuous review to examine the progress of the client at various stages of the recovery process. In practice, reviewing the client's progress is carried out across all phases in recovery and in Phase VII, a comprehensive review will be conducted. The purpose of the continuous review is to revisit the client's journey in recovery; acknowledge the progress/efforts made; and reaffirm the self-discovery, positive experiences, and the goals achieved by the client. It is a process of self-affirmation and self-reinforcement, providing positive energy for the client to carry on. In this chapter, the case of Ann will be used to illustrate the application of the Old Me/New Me and the Piggy Bank techniques in engaging the client in continuous review and feedback.

Intervention tool: Piggy Bank technique

Case background

The background of Ann's case was described in detail in Chapter 2 of this book.

Phase VII of Ann's recovery

Ann's life changed a lot after the first six stages of recovery. She was able to build up positive experiences, and identify internal and external resources and ways to use these resources for self-recovery. She had a good understanding of her thought pattern and dysfunctional cycle. Ann realized that she tended to fall into the thought trap of mind reading, thinking that others did not like her. Subsequently, she also learned to use the 5-Strategies to avoid falling into thought traps and the negative dysfunctional cycle.

In the previous stages, the worker constantly solicited and reviewed Ann's feedback. This action not only reviewed Ann's progress, but also helped to monitor Ann's feelings and responses closely. From Ann's perspective, she felt stuck in her old way of living. With new insight into the sources of her problems and clear steps to make improvement, her motivation to change had greatly increased. On the one hand, Ann was pleased with the changes because she then clearly realized that a change in her way of thinking could result in having different emotions and behaviours. On the other hand, this realization had aroused her desire to change other parts of her life, for example, to mend her conflictual interpersonal relationships.

After a client works through the different stages of recovery and makes significant improvements, it is still inevitable that he/she will continue to encounter many life challenges. It is therefore important for a client to be able to use the recently acquired knowledge and skills for continuous self-development and goal attainment. In the case of Ann, at the seventh stage, the focus of the intervention was to help her review the positive changes she had achieved in various stages of the recovery process, and to consolidate her experiences so that she could go forward with greater confidence and independence. The tools to be used included the Piggy Bank and Old Me/New Me techniques.

Concept and purpose of the technique

The Piggy Bank technique helps consolidate a client's abilities based on his/her successful real-life experiences. It also serves to reaffirm the client's achievements and strengths. The Piggy Bank technique, as the name suggests, 'saves up' the abilities and positive experiences of the client during the entire strength-based recovery process. At the final stage of recovery, the client can review the list of successful experiences stored in the Piggy Bank and consolidate the experiences and reaffirm his/her strengths and abilities. The following are some ways of identifying and building up positive experiences.

1   Through the Life Review Exercise (see Chapter 6), the client is helped to review abilities and strengths he/she has possessed since childhood and to explore real-life experiences to support and affirm those abilities and strengths. The identified successful experiences can be stored in the Piggy Bank.
2   During the strength-based recovery process, the worker can help the client identify his/her abilities and strengths in different life aspects. Experiences that affirm the client's abilities and strengths are then saved in the Piggy Bank.
3   The worker can also use the Behaviour Experiment technique and the Creating New Experiences technique described in Chapter 7 to create new positive experiences. These successful experiences can also be deposited in the Piggy Bank.

Operational procedure

During the early stages of the strength-based recovery process, the worker and the client will design a Piggy Bank together. This can be visualized as a checklist of successful experiences or can be individual notes that have been put inside a deposit box, or anything similar. Whenever a positive and successful experience is identified, the worker or the client will record it and deposit it into the Piggy Bank. At the final stage of the recovery process, the deposits inside the Piggy Bank will be taken out for a review to highlight the strengths and abilities of the client.

Saving and revisiting positive experiences are particularly important in the strength-based approach. With the passage of time and without proper recording of the positive experiences, the client and the worker will easily forget those experiences. This is especially meaningful for our clients because many of them tend to remember negative experiences while neglecting the positive ones. With this technique, the records kept in the Piggy Bank can be retrieved and be re-examined together with the client. At the same time, when the client begins to dwell on negative experiences or has doubts about his/her abilities and strengths, the worker can produce evidence to remind the client of his/her own abilities and strengths.

Case illustration

After saving for a period of time, the list in Ann's Piggy Bank showed the following:

WILLING TO LISTEN TO OTHERS' VIEWS

Evidence: When I encountered difficulties at work, I planned to resign. When the employer pointed out that resignation was evading the problem and advised me to take a break instead, I accepted the suggestion and stayed in the job.

HAVING THE COURAGE TO TRY

Evidence: Took initiative to communicate with housemates with whom I had a poor relationship, despite having the worry of being rejected.

HAVING ANALYTICAL POWER

Evidence: I reviewed my own changes together with the social worker. In facing life's challenges, I gathered views from different parties and conducted my own analysis.

EXPRESSING PERSONAL EMOTIONS APPROPRIATELY
INSTEAD OF THROWING A TANTRUM

Evidence: I communicated with housemates and house staff instead of making accusations and slamming the door, like I used to do.

MAKING THE BEST USE OF MY ARTISTIC TALENT

Evidence: Helped to decorate the hostel.

ABLE TO CALM MYSELF DOWN

Evidence: When I was in a bad mood, I calmed myself down in my room and got away from the difficult situation. I now often remind myself to think before taking any action.

WILLING TO CONSIDER THINGS FROM OTHERS' PERSPECTIVE

Evidence: I collaborated with my colleagues at work and accommodated their needs without thinking of them as nuisances.

HOLDING AN OPTIMISTIC AND THANKFUL ATTITUDE,
COUNTING MY BLESSINGS INSTEAD OF MY LOSSES

Evidence: In the past, I felt that staying in a halfway house was not my choice. I now realize that there are staff and roommates whom I can talk to and I feel happy about it.

Outcome

The Piggy Bank technique helped Ann realize strengths of which she was previously unaware. It also summed up her achievements in the recovery process. Ann stated that she would continue saving up her positive experiences and make good use of her abilities to sustain her efforts.

Reflection

The Piggy Bank technique can be used in conjunction with the Old Me/New Me technique (to be discussed in the next section). The Old Me/New Me technique elicits factual information from the client to examine his/her old and new self. For example, Ann used real-life experiences to illustrate how she used to avoid facing life's difficulties. In the New Me column, Ann reported that she now felt courageous and optimistic and the savings in the Piggy Bank could then be used as evidence to support her claim. The worker can assist the client in identifying evidence to support his/her change efforts from the Piggy Bank.

Intervention tool: Old Me/New Me

Case background

The same case, Ann, will be used to illustrate the use of the Old Me/New Me strategy.

Concept and purpose of the technique

Old Me/New Me is a SBCBT technique that aims to help a client revisit the positive changes and successful experiences gained in the recovery process, to consolidate what has been learned, and to build up his/her self-confidence. Through comparing the past and the present, the client can see clearly the various changes he/she has achieved and is able to evaluate him/herself in a positive light. This tool can also help the client in reviewing the trajectory of those changes.

Operational procedure

The worker invited Ann to describe her past and present behaviours using a worksheet (Worksheet 07), including how she managed challenging events and negative emotions, and how she had used different strategies that had brought different outcomes to her. Ann's descriptions follow.

Old Me

I used to avoid facing problems and tended to shift the responsibilities to others. I saw myself as having a lot of deficiencies and often felt helpless. Although I realized that this evasive attitude was not helping me to solve the problem, I was stuck in the dysfunctional cycle. My style in problem solving resulted in having multiple conflicts with others. I was often trapped in negative emotions. For example, when I heard different views from hostel staff, although it was possible for me to express my ideas, I was worried that I might end up having an emotional outburst and that the staff would evaluate my behaviour negatively. I always felt as though I were walking on thin ice and would try to escape under pressure. As a result, I missed many opportunities to communicate with others, and people would complain that they had difficulties understanding me.

New Me

Now I am willing to look at things from others' perspective. I have become more courageous and optimistic. For example, I am now willing to face and try to amend a conflictual relationship, taking the initiative to show my goodwill to those who have had poor relationships with me and to trying to communicate with them again. I also have begun to appreciate my own strengths. My mood has improved and I am more willing to communicate with others.

When reflecting on the process of the exercise, Ann realized that she rarely thought about or appreciated how she had changed, as she always felt that making changes was difficult and that she would do all she could to escape from difficult situations. Now that she found the root of the problem, she agreed that making changes was not as difficult as she had imagined and the outcomes were not necessarily negative. Furthermore, the affirmation and appreciation from people around became significant motivators for her to sustain her efforts.

Outcome

The biggest advantage of the Old Me/New Me technique is that it allows the client to articulate the changes him/herself. When he/she is willing to continue to adopt the New Me in conducting his/her life, he/she can visualize the positive outcomes, which serve as motivation to continue adopting it. This technique provides a concrete tool in comparing outcomes in using the new and old approaches and it helps the client to make smart choices towards the future.

Completing the Old Me/New Me worksheet brought a great sense of satisfaction and accomplishment for Ann. She could see results of her efforts and evidence of what she had achieved. After completing the worksheet, Ann was very pleased with herself and was amazed at what she had achieved via the New Me. She felt empowered, and the outcomes were what she had wanted. This gave Ann new hope and motivated her to stick to the new approach in the future.

In the recovery process, at times, Ann would revert to her previous pattern of doing things and start to have self-doubt. The worker had to remind her that it was normal to experience lapses in the recovery process. For instance, Ann expressed having work-related anxieties again, when without factual evidence, she suspected that her boss was pinpointing her. The worker immediately invited Ann to revisit the changes she described in the Old Me/New Me worksheet. Ann realized that she had once again fallen into a vicious cycle. The worksheet served as a reminder for Ann to avoid returning to the old pattern again.

Reflection

In the final stage of recovery, the goal is to help a client sustain his/her gains so that he/she can start to function independently in the New Me without the additional help of the worker. Therefore, it is very important to identify the client's motives and what the changes have meant for him/her. These are important elements to build up the client's New Me. For Ann, the motivation to change was that she did not want to evade difficult situations anymore and wanted to change her way of living. Changes for Ann also meant that she could make improvement in her emotions and interpersonal relationships, and pursue the longer-term goal of her recovery, having a stable job. Therefore, if the worker can help the client understand the motivation and significance of the changes, it can help to increase the client's determination in sustaining the efforts.

Conclusion

The final stage of the SBCBT on mental health recovery is the consolidation stage. It helps the client to see the achievements he/she has gained throughout the recovery process. One important message that needs to be clearly received and acknowledged by the client is that, it is his/her efforts that make the achievements possible. However, it is not uncommon to find clients who easily ascribe their successes to the efforts of the workers or other forces outside of themselves. This is why strategies such as the Piggy Bank and Old Me/New Me techniques are important and useful for providing concrete evidence of the gains made by the clients themselves, and not the workers, in the recovery process.

10 Application and reflection

Introduction

Having a severe mental illness is a major life challenge. It affects many aspects of one's life. Coupled with the prejudice present in the community, this may drastically change the sense of identity of the patient, causing him/her to lose hope and aspirations for the future. He/she may lose his/her life direction and goals and be confined in the trapped self. The concept of the strength-based cognitive behaviour therapy (SBCBT) approach to recovery highlights the liberation of self from a trapped state to a liberated state. It points out that the experience of mental illness should not be a reason for the client to lose hope and courage, as it is just a part of the person's life. On the other hand, the client can choose a positive attitude, educate him/herself on the illness, take the initiative to seek appropriate treatments, and learn to manage his/her lifestyle as well as physical and psychological health. Furthermore, the person can maintain a positive attitude towards personal dreams and aspirations, set personal goals and plans, and take actions towards achieving them. He/she can also learn to identify his/her own internal strengths and explore relevant external resources to pursue his/her dreams, and to build a rich and meaningful life. This is the road to recovery. This chapter collects the practice reflections made by colleagues who have participated in the SBCBT process, describing the joys and challenges they faced in carrying out the SBCBT approach in working with people in recovery.

However, this road to recovery is not an easy one. It is indeed not a simple task to transform from a trapped self to a liberated self. Recovery is a long journey and it requires a traveller to have courage, perseverance, positive thinking, constant hope, and willingness to try. Recovery can hardly be achieved by an individual alone. Support and guidance as well as companionship and encouragement of fellow travellers are essential. The role of a worker is also critical and meaningful in the road to recovery for the client. While embracing the recovery orientation in working with people with severe mental illness, a worker is constantly considering ways of encouraging, motivating, and providing guidance for the recovering person. Before the introduction of the strength-based model to recovery, some of the most common intervention approaches used for this target population were the rehabilitation model and the cognitive behavioural therapy (CBT). The current attempt to combine the strength-based model and CBT approach provides excellent experience and food for thought for our team of front-line social workers, and the following paragraphs delineate our thoughts and experiences in applying this SBCBT approach in the recovery of people with mental illness.

Experience and reflection

Complementariness of the recovery concept and cognitive behavioural therapy

A strength-based approach to mental health recovery emphasizes the exploration and utilization of personal strengths and external resources of the recovering person rather than focusing on the problem of an individual. Ironically, CBT has traditionally and conventionally been perceived as a problem-oriented approach, focusing on a client's problems and deficiencies. Throughout the application process, we repeatedly asked the question, 'How can CBT be combined with a strength-oriented approach?'. We believed that the two approaches could be complementary, but also acknowledged from the outset that the main thread of the intervention process was very much to be strength-based: helping an individual to set meaningful personal life goals, derive action plans, identify and use personal strengths and external resources to achieve the goals, and to overcome the personal and environmental obstacles to goal attainment. This direction set it apart from the problem-focused and deficit-focused approach inherent in traditional rehabilitation or CBT models.

From our practice experiences over the past two years, CBT can indeed be combined with a strength-based orientation in mental health recovery. Apart from the SBCBT model proposed by Padesky and Mooney (2012) (i.e., which is not specific to mental health recovery), our model is likely another major SBCBT model that provides a clear delineation of the phases and CBT techniques for working with people recovering from mental health concerns. It also has a strength assessment tool that helps to identify the various life domains that can be turned into goals and aspirations of the individual. In the Padesky and Mooney model, the ultimate concern is to facilitate an individual to become more resilient. Within the recovery context, we shift the focus from achieving resilience to one's meaning in life and life goals. These ultimate objectives are consistent with the concept of mental health recovery.

From the multitude of case illustrations found in this book, it is not difficult to see that there are obstacles to goal attainment that need to be addressed. One such obstacle is the dysfunctional emotional and behavioural responses that are commonly found in many clients with mental health concerns. Inadequate emotional management skills are found in many key aspects of a client's life, such as work, family, and interpersonal relationship.

CBT appears to be effective in addressing this obstacle. Take the example of Mrs. Ko described in previous chapters; her goals for recovery were to find a stable job and live independently. Through exploration, she also realized that her poor emotional management skills got in the way of her achieving the above goals because she often had poor relationships with her supervisors and colleagues at work. The Situational Self-Analysis exercise helped her see her illogical thinking and problems in attribution. In this case, CBT can help a client understand him/herself and the obstacle that is affecting his/her goal for recovery.

From a strength-based recovery perspective, the recovery process can be seen as a journey of self-discovery carried out purposefully by the client. In the recovery process, the client has a clear understanding of the illness and manages his/her own physical and psychological states conscientiously to prevent having a relapse. With hope and courage, the client tries new things for his/her personal growth; makes plans after understanding his/her hopes and aspirations; and builds up a support network for his/her recovery through developing interpersonal relationships. For CBT, a client's self-discovery is also central to the intervention process. The worker plays a facilitator role in assisting the client in recognizing his/her thinking and the interplay between thought, emotion, and behaviour, and their interaction with the environment. CBT also emphasizes a client's conscious choice of therapeutic goals and strategies in addressing his/her specific issues. When the client experiences positive changes through the newly developed strategies, the worker would help the client reflect on how the changes have happened and what can be done to continue with the success. All of these therapeutic elements can be directly adapted to the strength-based approach in mental health recovery. Indeed, through actual practices in the past two years, our workers have found more complementariness than we had anticipated in the concept of recovery and CBT.

Internalizing the strength perspective

The application of a strength perspective in recovery is a relatively new approach for mental health workers in Hong Kong. Mental health workers have long been trained to pay attention to the client's strengths and to encourage him/her to develop his/her strengths. However, before this project, many of us have not fully understood and appreciated the strength-based approach and how it can be practically applied in working with a client with mental health problems. Through this practice, we now understand that, in mental health recovery, the whole intervention process is guided by the principles of identifying the strengths of the client and removing barriers to goal achievement. However, an important insight that we have gained is that the worker him/herself must maintain a positive attitude and can internalize the strength perspective. During the intervention process, the worker must be alert to look for the positive qualities, abilities, interests, and characteristics of the client, both in the past and at present. In addition, in each successive intervention session, the worker must purposefully increase the positive experiences of the client. This can undoubtedly be an effective way to help a client recognize his/her uniqueness, and to enhance his/her sense of worth; both are fundamental core values of the recovery model.

Changing attitudes and roles of the workers

In the conventional rehabilitation model, the role of the worker is generally more directive in educating and providing guidance to the client to identify and solve problems. In contrast, under the recovery model, the worker and the client have a more equal relationship and work in partnership collaboratively. The worker provides support to the client and guides him/her towards self-discovery. What is important is that the client has to make his/her own choices, and the changes must be initiated by him/her. Indeed, the workers need to be conscientious in developing a new recovery lens in working with their clients in recovery. It is also important for workers to undergo regular supervision in order to fully acquire and internalize a strength-based recovery framework. This can and has posed a real challenge for some workers who are accustomed to a rehabilitation model. In sum, workers adopting the recovery model play a very different role from those using the CBT approach.

In our experience, some of the workers who participated in the project expressed concerns about exercising the new roles. For example, when helping the client in identifying obstacles (e.g., thought traps) that affected goal attainment, the workers were hesitant to point out the problems, particularly for clients who already had low self-confidence, and wondered how far they had to go to discuss problems with their clients. This is not an easy question to answer and we, as workers, have to work through it with each of our clients. Nonetheless, the overall principle is this: Strengths are our focus of intervention and we must try to help our client identify and develop his/her internal and external resources for attaining his/her goals. Indeed, it is a process that requires continuous reflection and attuning.

Issues with client's self-determination and goal setting

The recovery model emphasizes the autonomy of the client and the role of the worker as a working partner. Hence, the worker must respect the wishes of the client in setting and attaining his/her goals. However, it is not a simple task in practice.

For example, a young man who had participated in this project had the goal of becoming a singer and appeared to be highly insistent and committed to this dream. However, the worker had the impression that this was the client's way to avoid getting a job. Because he had no motivation to find a job, he spent a lot of time singing karaoke at home every day. His parents were extremely worried. The case worker frankly admitted that he was rather shocked at hearing the client's dream because the client did not seem to have the necessary vocal talent to become a singer. The worker felt that his dream was not realistic and that the worries of his parents should also be given consideration. The worker had to weigh carefully between following the wish of the client and making him face reality. Eventually, the worker decided on the former.

Another similar case involved a young female client who loved to do cosplay. She liked spending a lot of time dressing up and mimicking different cartoon characters. Her goal was to successfully play the role of her favourite comic book characters. The case worker was very doubtful at that time on whether this could be a working goal. From the worker's own perspective, the goal was unrealistic, and the conventional 'norm' in recovery is for a client to get a job and re-integrate into the community. On reflection, however, the worker realized that she should withhold her judgement of the client's wishes and should not allow her own values to interfere with the client's wish of achieving her goal. In addition, this judgemental attitude might also have posed a barrier to identifying the strengths of the client. With the renewed understanding on the meaning of starting where the client is, the worker started from the interest of the client (i.e., cosplay), and began to explore her personality traits, enabling her to gain self-confidence and recognize her own worth. Eventually, the worker also learned of the client's many other strengths when discussing cosplay with her. It turned out that although she seldom went out, she liked to communicate with people from other countries who were also interested in cosplay. Indeed, she had met some of these friends in Hong Kong and showed them around. On further exploration, the worker also found that apart from her interests in cosplay and Japanese culture, she also admired Japanese people's cleanliness and politeness. From her disclosure, the worker was able to understand her values and views. The worker then invited her to take a course on Japanese language at the centre. The client was able to build up her social circle and made friends with her peers. This gradually built up her confidence, and eventually, she was able to get a full-time job.

In another case, the initial goal of the client was to find a job. However, in the process of job seeking and maintenance, the client often avoided difficult situations and quickly gave up the job. Finally, she told the staff that she was satisfied with her current circumstance and would not look for a job. Financially, she was well supported by her husband and he did not have any strong preference for her to get a job. Another client had set the goal of expanding her social life. Although there were some improvements (e.g., she contacted her colleagues and had lunch with them), she felt that was good enough and had no intention to do more. From the above cases, the two major issues worth reflecting on are self-determination and goal setting.

First, concerning self-determination, it is one thing to acknowledge that we should respect our clients' choices. But when the choices appear to be unrealistic or, worse still, harmful to the physical and mental well-being of our clients, what should the workers do? Should we support or dissuade our clients from pursuing their dreams? How do we know if certain goals are unrealistic or even harmful for our clients? Honestly, we have not come up with the most satisfactory answers to the above questions. As recovery-oriented workers, we do adopt an openness to explore with our clients this sort of issue relating to self-determination. We will not push our clients to choose otherwise (i.e., although we may have our own preferences). Moreover, we accept the fact that clients can fail and have the right to fail and to learn from the failures. What is sometimes difficult for us is that the systems around our clients and us may not share the same sentiments and may lack similar levels of patience. Perhaps, this is a reality in life that our clients and we have to learn to deal with.

Regarding the issue of setting goals, first: if the dream of the client is unrealistic, should the worker respect his/her wishes without any intervention? After learning more about the case of the young man wishing to become a singer, the worker realized that factors affecting the client's decision to do so were partly due to his mental condition and partly due to the family dynamics. The parents of the client tended to be overprotective and accommodating to the client, which had resulted in his lack of confidence and motivation to grow up. During our intervention process, the client had actually made an attempt to find a job when his father was seriously ill. However, as soon as his father became physically better, the client returned to the old pattern of practicing singing all day again. After obtaining a more comprehensive picture of the situation, the worker understood that the client might be afraid to grow up. Helping him to build up confidence and develop abilities towards independent living became important components in his recovery. The lesson learned here is that the worker needs to understand the psychological struggle behind the client's lack of motivation to develop realistic life goals.

Second, it is important for the worker to explore what the dream means to the client. The young person who dreamed of becoming a singer wished to encourage and inspire others through his songs. This also matched with his underlying wish to become a successful and useful person to be recognized particularly by his parents (i.e., we found this out through conversations he had about his famous comic book). The woman who initially had the dream of finding a job but later decided not to do so actually wanted to become a useful person but was lacking the confidence to cope with work stress. The dream of another client (i.e., not mentioned above) was to get a subsidized flat through compassionate rehousing (i.e., a Hong Kong government housing scheme for people in need). For her, a flat meant a stable life, which would be very different from her previous pattern of living. In sum, it is essential to explore and understand the underlying meaning of the client's dream, and to communicate such understanding with the client. Once the client feels understood, the worker can explore and expand the client's options to achieve the same dream, and thus, increase the likelihood of success for the client.

'Problems' in the context of the strength-based recovery approach

Before adopting the recovery model, when helping a client with mental illness, our workers had used different intervention approaches under the umbrella term of casework and individual counselling. In general, the worker would collect detailed information on a client's family background and personal history. The worker would then assess the information and try to identify the predisposing factors, precipitating factors, perpetuating factors, and protective factors surrounding the client's presenting problem. After conceptualizing the case, the worker would gain more understanding of the development and maintenance of the client's problem and then formulate a treatment plan.

In the SBCBT approach, the issues at hand are not necessarily perceived as problems. They are areas of concern, yearnings, or wishes that can potentially be developed into goals that can further be fulfilled through the employment of one's internal and external resources. The main focus of intervention is on exploring strengths and wishes. After exploring what internal and external resources the client possesses, the worker assists the client in formulating his/her goals and action plan. The worker would also carefully facilitate the client to execute the plan. However, can we forgo the 'problems' that are faced by our clients and just focus on developing strengths? How can client problems be understood under a SBCBT approach?

Our experience tells us that when using a SBCBT approach, 'problems' (e.g., severity of the psychiatric symptoms, difficulties with housing, and family conflicts) can be meaningfully translated into underlying concerns, yearnings, or wishes that can potentially be developed into goals for future attainment. In addition, 'problems' can also be conceptualized as obstacles (e.g., internal obstacles such as dysfunctional pattern of responses and external obstacles such as lack of community resources) that hinder the client from achieving his/her goals. The worker should explore the client's background and experience, and also try to understand the internal and external obstacles that are affecting the situation. When providing services for a client using the SBCBT approach, the worker must be cognizant of both the strengths and the problems being experienced by the client. Both aspects are important in the intervention process.

Conclusion

Mental illness brings negative emotions, negative experiences, and impairments to a client. In a way, the person is trapped in those negativities. SBCBT intends to facilitate an individual with mental illness to move from the trapped self to liberated self. By combining a recovery perspective and CBT, the approach provides a positive and strength-oriented basis in helping the client to build a meaningful and purposeful life. The techniques in CBT can also be modified to become strength-focused.

11 Outcomes of strength-based cognitive behaviour therapy for people recovering from mental illness

Introduction

This chapter introduces the research process (and its outcomes) that were built in this project of applying strength-based cognitive behaviour therapy (SBCBT) in working with people recovering from mental illness. The project was guided by our self-developed working model, called 'SET', with S standing for services for our clients, E meaning evaluation, and T denoting training. Throughout the project, the participating social workers underwent training in SBCBT organized by the first author and his team at the University of Hong Kong. The workers also received monthly group supervision from the research and training team. After the initial training, the participating agency recruited clients with mental health concerns to participate in this one-year intervention. A research component was also built into the project to examine the effectiveness of the intervention on clients' changes in mental health and recovery-oriented outcomes. Below are the research project details, including objectives, methods, results, and discussion and recommendations. The full contents have been published in Research on Social Work Practice Online First version on October 13, 2017. DOI: 10.1177/1049731517732837.

Aims and objectives

Meta-analyses of overseas studies have found that (1) there is insufficient concluding evidence to support the effectiveness of recovery-oriented approaches in working with people with mental illness; (2) there is a lack of clear documentation of how the recovery principles and techniques have been actualized in the implementation process in working with people with mental health concerns, and (3) all of the chosen studies in the two available meta-analyses, albeit small in numbers, were conducted in Western cultures and it is understood that the conceptualization and expression of emotions and strengths are heavily influenced by culture (Ibrahim, Michail, & Callaghan, 2014; Tse et al., 2016).

A browse through the literature found only two articles on the application and evaluation of the effectiveness of a strength-based recovery-oriented program for Chinese people. The first study was a qualitative research that interviewed 13 Chinese clients in New Zealand who had gone through a recovery intervention process using wellness recovery action planning (WRAP) over a three-month period (Zhang, Li, Yeh, Wong, & Zhao, 2007). Broadly speaking, the results suggested that WRAP made a significant role in the recovery of these clients. The second study was a quantitative one that evaluated the effectiveness of WRAP in a matched controlled design among individuals in recovery of mental illness in Hong Kong (Mak et al., 2016). The participants went through the group WRAP program in eight consecutive weeks. The results indicated that compared to their matched controls, WRAP participants reported significant increases in perceived social support. However, no significant change was noted in empowerment, hope, self-stigma, social network size, symptom severity, and recovery.

In Hong Kong, there has been a gradual shift towards a recovery approach in mental health care among service providers in hospital and community psychiatric settings. However, the development and implementation of recovery practices are still in their infancy, and there is a lack of a clear set of culturally attuned strategies that are empirically tested to actualize the process of recovery for people with mental illness in Hong Kong (Tse, Siu, & Kan, 2013). Indeed, as Tse et al. (2013) assert, recovery is a culturally bounded concept interpreted differently across cultures, and thus must be understood within a cultural context (Tse, Cheung, Kan, Ng, & Yau, 2012; Tse et al., 2013). Although various agencies in Hong Kong have adopted recovery-oriented case management in working with people with severe mental illnesses (SMIs), there are at least two issues concerning its application in Hong Kong. First, there is an absence of a localized model of recovery with a clear delineation of specific skills/techniques. Second, there is an absence of any clinical data that support the positive effects of a culturally adapted recovery-oriented model for Hong Kong Chinese. This project has attempted to fill these gaps.

The objective of our study was to examine the effects of a strength-based cognitive behaviour therapy in enhancing the mental health, hope, feelings of empowerment, and quality of life of people with SMI. It is hypothesized that the participants of the experimental group would show continuous improvement in self-assessed recovery, hope, quality of life, and mental health when compared to the participants of the control group from pretest, 6 months, and 12 months of intervention.

Method

Participants

Nine social workers from Baptist Oi Kwan Social Services Organization (BOKSS), a local social service agency in Hong Kong, were involved in this project. Because both CBT programs and recovery-oriented interventions were reported to have an overall medium mean effect sizes (Ibrahim et al., 2014;

Wilson, Bouffard, & Mackenzie, 2005), sample size was calculated based on a conservative expectation of an effect size of 0.25 for the present recovery-oriented CBT program. The minimum sample size was calculated by G*power 3.1.3. For 80% power, an α error of 0.05 and a test of two independent groups, the total required number was 40. Therefore, each participating social worker was required to recruit three pairs of experimental and matched-pair control subjects. The inclusion criteria were: (1) aged between 18 and 60 years; (2) a clinical diagnosis of severe mental disorder, such as depression, bipolar, schizophrenia, or obsessive-compulsive disorder; (3) new service user (0–6 months) of BOKSS Wellness Centre (i.e., a local mental health social service agency in Hong Kong); (4) mentally stable at the time of recruitment; and (5) able to self-complete the questionnaire. The matched pair criteria were: (1) same gender, (2) similar age (+/– 3 years), (3) same diagnosis, and (4) similar length of time of having the mental disorder (+/– 3 years). Finally, there were 27 and 25 participants recruited in the experimental and control groups respectively. Two participants from the control group withdrew from the project due to a lack of interest in the services.

Procedure.

Ethical approval of this study was granted by the ethics committee of City University of Hong Kong. A thorough introduction of the study was provided for each eligible participant by the respective social worker. After obtaining an informed consent from each participant, the social worker involved provided recovery-oriented cognitive-behaviour service approach for the participants in the experimental group, while the other social workers provided standard counselling service without the recovery-oriented cognitive-behaviour approach for participants in the control group. All participants were given a battery of self-administered instruments including basic demographics and outcome assessments. An independent researcher collected the questionnaires at three time points including pre-intervention, 6-month assessment, and 12-month assessment (Figure 11.1).

Contents of the intervention

EXPERIMENTAL GROUP

The participants in the experimental group received regular monthly individual counselling using a SBCBT approach as the medium of intervention, and each session lasted for one hour. The counselling process followed the seven stages of the recovery model, which included: instilling hope and motivation; identifying needs; developing goals; exploring internal and external resources; developing tasks, strategies and plans; identifying personal and environment barriers; and engaging in ongoing evaluation. Specific cognitive and behavioural exercises and techniques were used at each stage of the recovery process.

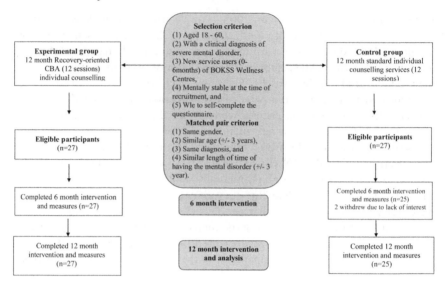

Figure 11.1 Flow diagram of the intervention through the stages of the study.

The entire process took an average of about one year to complete. The demographics of participants by group are presented in Table 11.1.

CONTROL GROUP

The participants in the control group received individual case management (i.e., treatment as usual) from social workers who did not partake in the SBCBT training and intervention project. Case management is a collaborative process of assessment, planning, facilitation, care coordination, evaluation, and advocacy for options and services to meet an individual's and family's comprehensive health needs through communication and available resources to promote quality, cost-effective outcomes (Department of Health, Australia 2017). The participants and their families received support from social workers who assessed their needs, helped them set short-term and long-term goals, coordinated their treatment plans, and connected them with the resources they needed to successfully manage their conditions on their own. The case management model that was adopted was problem-oriented, addressing the deficits faced by the control group participants in the rehabilitation process.

Treatment fidelity

All social workers participating in the study were registered social workers with a minimum of three years of experience in delivering mental

Table 11.1 Demographics of participants by group

		Control group (N=25)	Experimental group (N=27)
		n (%)	*n (%)*
Gender	Male	3 (12.00)	4 (14.80)
	Female	22 (88.00)	23 (96.30)
Age	Mean (SD)	40.36 (11.19)	39.11 (11.83)
Marital status	Single	15 (60.00)	16 (59.30)
	Married	7 (28.00)	4 (14.80)
	Separated/Divorced	2 (8.00)	4 (14.80)
	Widowed	1 (4.00)	2 (7.40)
	Other	–	1 (3.70)
Education	Primary or below	1 (4.00)	1 (3.70)
	Primary	3 (12.00)	1 (3.70)
	Secondary	4 (16.00)	8 (29.60)
	Completed secondary	6 (24.00)	5 (18.50)
	Preparatory course	2 (8.00)	3 (11.10)
	Tertiary and above	9 (36.00)	9 (33.30)
Employment	Full time	8 (32.00)	6 (22.20)
	Housewife	5 (20.00)	3 (11.10)
	Student	–	1 (3.70)
	Part–time	3 (12.00)	5 (18.50)
	Unemployed	8 (32.00)	11 (40.70)
	Retired	1 (4.00)	1 (3.70)
Illness (some participants with multiple diagnoses)	Schizophrenia	7 (28.00)	8 (29.60)
	Bipolar disorder	3 (12.00)	5 (18.50)
	Mania	–	–
	Psychosis	7 (28.00)	6 (22.20)
	Delusion disorder	–	2 (7.40)
	Depression	8 (32.00)	8 (29.60)
Duration of diagnosis	Mean (SD)	8.58 (7.04)	9.65 (8.03)
Consultation	No consultation	–	1 (3.70)
	Yes but unstable	1 (4.00)	3 (11.10)
	Yes and stable	24 (96.00)	23 (85.20)
Medication	Yes and stable	24 (96.00)	25 (92.60)
	Yes but unstable	–	2 (7.40)
	No required under medical advice	1 (4.00)	
Frequency of hospital admittance in past 6 months	0	22 (88.00)	24 (88.90)
	1	3 (12.00)	2 (7.40)
	2	–	1 (3.70)
Average number of days in hospital in past 6 months (answered above only)	Mean (SD)	2.44 (8.29)	8.93 (38.95)

health services for the target participants. In the beginning of the project, all involved social workers received a three-day training in the recovery model and cognitive behaviour therapy (CBT). An experienced mental health academic who is also a certified cognitive therapist, trained at the Beck Institute of Cognitive Therapy, provided the training and the monthly group supervision for the involved social workers, while the agency supervisors of BOKSS Wellness Centres also rendered monthly individual supervision.

Instruments

MENTAL HEALTH RECOVERY MEASURE (YOUNG & BULLOCK, 2005)

The Mental Health Recovery Measure (MHRM) is a self-report instrument that aims at comprehensively assessing the recovery process of individuals with SMIs. This measure consists of 30 items and is rated on a five-point Likert scale ranging from 0 (strongly disagree) to 4 (strongly agree). This scale contains seven domains including overcoming stuckness, self-empowerment, learning and self-redefinition, basic functioning, overall well-being, finding new potentials, and advocacy/enrichment. Each domain comprises four items. The higher the summary score, the more the respondent has recovered from the illness. The Chinese version of this measure has been translated and validated by the principal investigator and his associates and has been used in previous research (Ye, Pan, Wong, & Bola, 2013). This scale achieved high internal consistency in this study (pre-intervention = 0.91, 6-month intervention = 0.96, 12-month intervention = 0.93).

RECOVERY SELF-ASSESSMENT REVISED (ORDE,
CHAMBERLIN, CARPENTER, & LEFF, 2005).

The Recovery Self-Assessment Revised (RSA-R) was developed to evaluate recovery-oriented practices in a mental health service. The RSA-R contains 32 items and constitutes five subscales that measure the domains of life goals, involvement, diversity of treatment options, choice, and individually tailored services. All items are rated using the five-point Likert scale that ranges from 1 (strongly disagree) to 5 (strongly agree). The option of 'not applicable' is also included in each item. The higher the summary score, the more recovery-oriented practice a service is perceived to be providing. The Chinese version of this measure has been translated and validated by the principal investigator and his associates and has been used in previous research (Ye et al., 2013). This scale achieved high internal consistency in this study (pre-intervention = 0.93, 6-month intervention = 0.70, 12-month intervention = 0.88).

The WHOQOL-BREF (HK) consists of 28 items. The first two items are global questions, asking respondents to rate their overall quality of life (Q1) and overall health condition (Q2). The remaining 26 items cover the domains with regard to physical, psychological, social, and environmental aspects of quality of life of the respondent. The measure uses a five-point Likert scale that ranges from 1 (very dissatisfied) to 5 (very satisfied). The WHOQOL-BREF (HK) was validated and used for evaluating long-term outcome of patients who are living in the community. Higher summary scores denote better subjective well-being of the respondent. This scale achieved high internal consistency in the present study (pre-intervention = 0.88, 6-month intervention = 0.92, 12-month intervention = 0.90).

The Trait Hope Scale consists of 12 items, exploring dispositional or trait-like hope of a respondent. Four items measure pathway thinking and another four assess agentic thinking. The remaining four items are distracters and are not scored. Respondents are asked to rate the degree to which they believe in each statement (ranging from 1 = definitely false to 8 = definitely true). The scores of agency and pathway thinking may be summed to create a total hope score with a higher score indicating a higher level of hope in recovery. The scale was reported to have adequate internal reliability and temporal reliability. It was translated into Chinese and the Cronbach's alpha of the Chinese version was 0.85 (Ho, Ho, Bonanno, Chu, & Chan, 2010). This scale achieved high internal consistency in the current study (pre-intervention = 0.87, 6-month intervention = 0.89, 12-month intervention = 0.84).

Statistical analysis

Data analyses were performed on an intention-to-treat principle, with the missing data for each outcome measure inputted using 'last observation carried forward'. Differences in each demographic variable between the experimental and control groups at pre-test were examined using chi-square analyses for categorical variables and analyses of variance (ANOVAs) for continuous variables. Age and years of diagnosis of participants were treated as covariates as some participants exceeded the matched pair criteria. A series of 2 × 3 repeated measures ANOVAs were performed to examine the main and interaction effects of time and group on the outcome measures at pre-intervention, and at 6-month and 12-month intervention. Cohen's d was used to measure the magnitude of change in outcome variables between pre-intervention and 6-month intervention and between pre-intervention and 12-month intervention in both experimental and control groups (Cohen, 1988). Regression analyses were also applied to examine the effects of the perceived changes in hope and recovery-oriented practices in a mental health service on changes in quality of life and self-perceived recovery measures of the participants.

Results

In the experimental group, the majority, around 96%, were women, with a mean age of 39.11 years (SD = 12.83). Around 59% of participants were single and 33% received tertiary education or above. Most participants (around 41%) were unemployed. An equal number of participants were diagnosed with depression or schizophrenia, whilst the average year since diagnosis was 9.65 years. The majority of the participants had not been hospitalized in the past six months and received regular consultation and were under stable medication (Table 11.1).

For the control group, the majority (around 88%) were women with a mean age of 40.36 years (SD = 11.19). In addition, 60% were single and 36% received tertiary education or above. An equal number of participants were involved in full-time jobs or were unemployed. The most popular diagnoses amongst the participants were depression, schizophrenia, or psychosis. The majority of the participants had not been hospitalized in the past six months, all received consultation, and the majority were under stable medication (Table 11.1).

Chi-square and ANOVAs (two-tailed) were used to test for demographic differences in the experimental and control groups, whereas ANOVAs (two-tailed) were used to test for baseline differences in outcome variables between groups. No significant baseline differences ($ps > 0.05$) were found for outcome measures as well as demographic variables; thus both groups were found comparable. The means and standard deviations of outcome measures of both the experimental and control groups are presented in Table 11.2.

Mental health recovery

A 2 × 3 repeated measures ANOVA (two-tailed) revealed that there were significant time × group interaction effects in the Mental Health Recovery functional subscale ($F = 3.97$, $p = 0.03$), new potential subscale ($F = 4.14$, $p = 0.02$), spirituality subscale ($F = 3.37$, $p = 0.05$), and total score ($F = 3.73$, $p = 0.03$) (Table 11.3). Because interaction effects were significant, simple main effects, using the Bonferroni adjustment were conducted. The experimental group revealed significant improvements in the basic functioning subscale ($F = 9.05$, $p < 0.001$) between pre-intervention and 12-month intervention ($p = 0.01$) (Cohen's d = 0.58), whilst the control group was insignificant ($F = 1.75$, $p = 0.19$) in the opposite direction. As for the new potentials subscale, the experimental group revealed significant improvements ($F = 9.42$, $p < 0.001$) between pre-intervention and 6-month intervention ($p < 0.001$) (Cohen's d = 0.73) and between pre-intervention and 12-month intervention

Table 11.2 Mean and standard deviations of outcome variables by group

Control Group N=25	Pre-test		6-month			12-month		
	M	SD	M	SD		M	SD	
Mental health recovery measure								
Overcoming stuckness	15.92	1.73	16.28	2.09		16.16	1.70	
Self-empowerment	14.00	2.12	14.76	2.71		14.60	2.40	
Learning and self-redefinition	15.00	2.24	15.00	2.40		15.40	1.55	
Basic functioning	14.20	2.08	13.76	2.40		14.00	1.98	
Overall well-being	13.96	2.07	14.36	2.80		14.00	2.55	
New potentials	13.24	2.49	13.40	3.19		13.84	2.62	
Spirituality	7.08	1.47	6.72	1.74		7.00	1.96	
Advocacy	13.04	2.35	13.00	2.93		13.44	3.01	
Total	100.12	11.20	107.28	16.57		108.44	13.75	
Recovery self-assessment revised								
Lifegoal	3.95	0.70	3.88	0.63		3.88	0.64	
Involvement	3.51	1.10	3.48	0.86		3.33	0.62	
Treatment diversity	3.57	1.11	3.49	0.93		3.58	0.69	
Choice	4.00	0.72	3.80	0.75		3.15	0.60	
Individual tailor services	3.72	0.87	3.72	0.61		3.70	0.71	
Total	3.86	0.74	3.76	0.60		3.79	0.55	
Quality of life								
Physical	21.93	3.44	21.92	3.76		22.08	3.45	
Psychological	17.42	3.26	17.36	4.11		17.92	3.26	
Social	11.87	2.36	11.63	2.66		12.04	2.54	
Environment	29.80	4.78	29.00	5.51		29.48	5.10	
Total	81.01	10.99	79.91	13.96		81.52	12.15	
Hope scale								
Agency	19.04	5.78	19.00	5.20		19.68	5.42	
Pathway	19.15	4.88	18.64	4.53		19.28	5.26	
Total	32.91	8.53	37.64	8.78		38.96	9.72	

(Continued)

Table 11.2 Mean and standard deviations of outcome variables by group (Continued)

Experimental Group N=27	Pre-test		6-month		12-month	
	M	SD	M	SD	M	SD
Mental health recovery measure						
Overcoming stuckness	15.85	1.77	16.41	1.95	16.44	1.60
Self-empowerment	14.26	2.43	15.30	2.88	14.53	2.95
Learning and self-redefinition	14.44	2.52	15.72	2.12	15.93	2.22
Basic functioning	13.81	2.22	14.70	2.23	15.11	2.31
Overall wellbeing	13.15	3.08	14.26	3.05	14.41	2.55
New potentials	12.56	3.23	14.81	3.06	14.48	3.44
Spirituality	7.07	1.17	7.78	1.63	7.78	1.84
Advocacy	13.44	2.22	14.11	2.38	14.00	2.13
Total	98.04	13.62	113.09	16.62	112.68	13.83
Recovery self-assessment revised						
Lifegoal	3.88	0.51	3.94	0.65	4.10	0.46
Involvement	3.74	0.81	3.86	0.67	3.84	0.56
Treatment diversity	3.74	0.70	4.10	1.73	3.81	0.65
Choice	3.95	0.67	3.98	0.62	3.31	0.36
Individual tailor services	3.73	0.66	3.97	0.65	4.02	0.51
Total	3.85	0.53	3.97	0.63	4.04	0.42
Quality of life						
Physical	20.97	5.07	22.78	4.27	22.41	4.17
Psychological	16.74	4.35	17.63	3.90	18.04	3.67
Social	12.00	2.56	12.19	1.94	12.37	2.06
Environment	28.26	4.44	28.38	4.20	28.57	4.67
Total	77.97	13.98	80.98	11.58	81.38	11.81
Hope scale						
Agency	19.81	4.99	21.22	4.58	21.93	4.19
Pathway	19.74	5.32	21.59	4.89	22.41	3.99
Total	34.19	8.17	42.81	9.04	44.33	7.30

Table 11.3 Interaction effects and group effects by outcome variables

	Interaction effects (time*group)		Between group effects		Cohen's d treatment group	Cohen's d treatment group
					Pre vs. 6-month	Pre vs. 12-month
	F	p	F	p		
Mental health recovery measure						
Overcoming stuckness	0.48	0.62	0.12	0.73	0.43	0.36
Self-empowerment	0.56	0.57	0.06	0.81	0.40	0.10
Learning and self-redefinition	3.06	0.06	0.18	0.68	0.56	0.64v
Basic functioning	3.97	0.03*	0.39	0.54	0.41	0.58
Overall well-being	1.76	0.18	0.11	0.75	0.37	0.45
New potentials	4.14	0.02*	0.39	0.54	0.73	0.59
Spirituality	3.37	0.05*	2.49	0.12	0.51	0.47
Advocacy	0.52	0.47	1.11	0.30	0.30	0.26
Total	3.73	0.03*	0.85	0.36	1.01	1.09
Recovery self-assessment revised						
Lifegoal	1.77	0.18	0.60	0.44	0.10	0.46
Involvement	0.78	0.45	5.28	0.02*	0.16	0.15
Treatment diversity	1.18	0.31	2.88	0.10	0.28	0.11
Choice	1.03	0.35	0.89	0.35	0.05	1.21
Individual tailor services	2.00	0.15	2.27	0.14	0.37	0.49
Total	1.87	0.17	1.81	0.19	0.51	0.40
Quality of life						
Physical	1.50	0.23	0.01	0.92	0.39	0.32
Psychological	0.76	0.47	0.17	0.69	0.22	0.33
Social	0.37	0.64	0.44	0.51	0.09	0.16
Environment	0.58	0.56	0.95	0.34	0.03	0.07
Total	1.50	0.23	15	0.70	0.24	0.27
Hope scale						
Agency	1.46	0.24	1.91	0.17	0.30	0.45
Pathway	3.20	0.05*	3.78	0.06	0.37	0.58
Total	3.24	0.05*	3.34	0.07	1.02	1.34

$\star$ $p < 0.05$

($p < 0.001$) (Cohen's d = 0.59); whilst control group was insignificant ($F = 0.56$, $p = 0.58$). Furthermore, for the spirituality subscale, the experimental group showed significant improvements at 6-month of intervention only ($F = 5.51$, $p = 0.03$) (Cohen's d = 0.51), whilst the control group displayed changes in the opposite direction. Also there were significant differences between the experimental group and control group at 6-month intervention ($F = 5.507$, $p < 0.05$) (Cohen's d = 0.62). As for the total score, there were improvements both in the experimental ($F = 22.54$, $p < 0.001$) and control group ($F = 5.77$, $p = 0.01$). Improvements in the experimental group were significant between pre-intervention and 6-month intervention ($p < 0.001$) (Cohen's d = 1.01) and between pre-intervention and 12-month intervention ($p < 0.001$) (Cohen's d = 1.09), whilst control group was only significant between pre-intervention and 12-month intervention ($p < 0.001$). The experimental group reported a significant improvement in mental health recovery while the control group took longer to improve.

Recovery self-assessment (revised) and quality of life
scale — Chinese version (WHOQOL-BREF)

A 2 × 3 repeated measures ANOVA (two-tailed) revealed that there were no significant time × group interaction effects in the recovery self-assessment (revised) subscales as well as total scores (Table 11.3). However, simple effect tests showed that the experimental group had significant within-group differences at 6-month intervention ($F = 4.37$, $p = 0.042$) (Cohen's d = 0.49) and 12-month intervention ($F = 11.05$, $p = 0.002$) (Cohen's d = 0.86) concerning the involvement subscale. People in the experimental group reported feeling more involved in learning about recovery, and felt that they could contribute to society as well as program evaluation in the agency.

A 2 × 3 repeated measures ANOVA (two-tailed) revealed that there were no significant time × group interaction effects in the quality of life subscales as well as total score (Table 11.3). The results also showed no significant between-group effects (Table 11.3). Simple effect tests showed there was no significant difference between the experimental group and control group across three time points.

Adult hope scale

A 2 × 3 repeated measures ANOVA (two-tailed) revealed that there were significant time × group interaction effects in the adult hope scale pathway subscale (Table 11.3) ($F = 3.20$, $p = 0.05$) and total score ($F = 3.24$, $p = 0.05$). Because interaction effects were significant, simple main effects, using the Bonferroni adjustment were conducted. As for pathway thinking subscale, the experimental group showed significant improvements at 6-month intervention ($F = 4.69$, $p = 0.04$) (Cohen's d = 0.37) and 12-month intervention ($F = 5.73$, $p = 0.02$) (Cohen's d = 0.58). The experimental group reported feeling significantly more planned in achieving goals at 6-month and 12-month intervention. The comparison between the experimental group and control group showed there were significant differences at 6-month intervention ($F = 5.77$, $p = 0.02$) (Cohen's d = 0.63) and 12-month intervention ($F = 5.73$, $p = 0.02$) (Cohen's d = 0.67). People in the experimental group showed more pathway thinking. Moreover for the total score, the experimental group showed significant improvements at 6-month intervention ($F = 4.69$, $p = 0.04$) (Cohen's d = 1.02) and 12-month intervention ($F = 4.84$, $p = 0.03$) (Cohen's d = 1.34). Also, there were significant differences between the experimental and control group at 6-month intervention ($F = 4.684$, $p = 0.035$) (Cohen's d = 0.58) and 12-month intervention ($F = 4.836$, $p = 0.03$) (Cohen's d = 0.62). The experimental group has better results than the control group. The experimental group reported feeling significantly more hopeful about the future at 6-month and 9-month interventions.

Discussion

Effects of culturally attuned recovery-oriented CBA for Chinese people with mental illness

Our study provides initial evidence towards the effects of a SBCBT approach in improving Hong Kong Chinese participants' overall basic mental health functioning and in the feelings of having more new potentials and greater spirituality in mental recovery. These findings echo those in the Western literature, which support the effectiveness of recovery-oriented approaches in enhancing the psychological well-being, self-identity, self-esteem, and meaning in life among individuals who have received recovery-oriented services (Andresen, Oades, & Caputi, 2003). However, this is the first study that provides clear evidence towards the application of a culturally attuned recovery-oriented approach in helping ethnic groups with mental health concerns, such as the Chinese. To begin with, all SBCBT exercises and worksheets (i.e., recovery-oriented needs assessment form, the auction game of life—identifying future aspirations, event charting—exploring past successful experiences, implementing specific life goals: a step-by-step process, strengths list/piggy bank technique, exposure/behavioural experiment) have been written or translated into Chinese so that the mental health workers and clients can easily understand and use the exercises and worksheets. A three-day training on the use of this SBCBT was organized to help familiarize mental health workers with this approach. In addition, monthly supervision was given by the first author to all participating mental health workers for the entire period (i.e., 18 months) of the implementation of the project. Although this study did not purposefully examine issues concerning the cultural application of a Western approach, mental health workers who used this approach expressed in a feedback session their appreciation of the availability of locally translated and written worksheets and exercises (i.e., commonly found in a CBT approach) that they could readily use to work with their clients. To echo the idea suggested by Tse et al. (2016), the conceptualization and expression of emotions and strengths are heavily influenced by culture, and therefore, it is necessary to develop culturally sensitive recovery-oriented strengths-based practices that would blend into the cultural characteristics of the specific cultural group.

Importance of planning in achieving goals and instilling hope

This study appears to suggest that the participants who went through our SBCBT intervention had a greater sense of hope, particularly in terms of pathway (i.e., hopeful about planning to accomplish goals), and greater improvements in the overall mental health functioning, particularly in spirituality and new potentials (i.e., the latter concerns setting and achieving goals). In the intervention process, mental health workers used different SBCBT tools (e.g., Strengths Assessment form, auction game of life—identifying future aspirations, event charting—exploring past successful experiences, implementing specific life goals: a step-by-step process) to facilitate the participants to develop and implement their goals. Moreover, several techniques such as validating the strengths of the client and the strengths list/Piggy Bank techniques were used to help the individual participants to examine, appreciate, and validate their positive gains. These tools might have been able to facilitate the person to develop and achieve his/her goals. In turn, with repeated positive results, this process might have instilled a sense of hope in the participant. As our study also indicates, an increasing sense of hope among participants, whether they were in the experimental or control group, was predictive of their positive changes in mental health recovery and quality of life. Indeed, Clarke and colleagues (2009) found that consumers who made greater progress in their goals and reported an elevated sense of self-confidence in achieving future goals were more hopeful about their future and had an increased sense of identity and purpose in life.

Importance of consumer participation in the recovery process

Our study appears to provide some initial support that our SBCBT was able to enhance a general sense of increased consumer involvement in the recovery process among the participants in the experimental condition while the participants in the control condition made no significant changes in such consumer involvement. This is an encouraging note because, as Marshall, Crowe, Oades, Deane, and Kavanagh (2007) have suggested, greater consumer involvement is essential for personal recovery, with the consumers being able to articulate what they see as important and meaningful for their recovery process. Moreover, a sense of involvement also signifies the fact that a consumer's view is honoured and respected (Torrey, Rapp, Van Tosh, McNabb, & Ralph, 2005). Indeed, the findings of our study support the importance of personal involvement in impacting basic functioning and mental health recovery and quality of life of the participants in the experimental group while no such significant impact was observed in the control group.

Limitations

Although our study demonstrates preliminary results regarding the positive effects of our SBCBT intervention in Hong Kong, we need to be aware of several limitations. First, this is an initial systematic study with a relatively small sample size. A larger sample size is needed in future study to provide more robust evidence supporting the model's positive effects. Second, the robustness of this study can be further enhanced by introducing a randomized control design in order to minimize various biases such as Hawthorne and John Henry effects. Lastly, we cannot rule out the possibility that positive changes in the various outcome measures at 6-month and 12-month interventions might have been due to confounding factors (e.g., therapist style) other than the intervention itself. Future studies might want to include these as covariates in the analysis.

Conclusion

This chapter includes a study that provided preliminary evidence about the positive effects of the SBCBT approach for Chinese people with SMI in Hong Kong. The results show that this approach could significantly enhance the mental health (especially basic functioning, finding new potentials, spirituality, and total score) and sense of hope among Chinese people with SMI in Hong Kong. Given these possible advantages, it is necessary to conduct further and more vigorous trials of this intervention approach to ascertain its clear benefits. Moreover, training and supervision for mental health workers are needed in order to ensure that mental health professionals have acquired the correct attitudes and skills to carry out this SBCBT approach.

Appendix
Worksheets

Worksheet 01 Situational Self-Analysis exercise

Precipitating event	Physical response	Emotional response	Behavioural response	Thought	Thought trap

Name: _____ Date: _____

Worksheet 02 Life Goal Formulation Chart

My life goal priorities

Number 1: Hope to achieve most; ... Number 5: Does not matter much even if not able to achieve

Priority	Life goal	Reason
Number 1		
Number 2		
Number 3		
Number 4		
Number 5		

(Continued)

Worksheet 02 Life Goal Formulation Chart (*Continued*)

My goals

Goal	Action plan
Goal 1	
Goal 2	
Goal 3	

My action plan in achieving my goals

Goal	Action plan	Outcome indicator	Timeline	Self-reinforcement

Worksheet 03 Life Review Exercise

Please recall events that made you happy, gave you a sense of accomplishment, and gave you a deep impression in different stages of your life. Record the events briefly in the table below.

Childhood	*Adolescence*
Event 1	Event 1
Underlying meaning	Underlying meaning
Event 2	Event 2
Underlying meaning	Underlying meaning

(Continued)

Adulthood	Elderly
Event 1	Event 1
Underlying meaning	Underlying meaning
Event 2	Event 2
Underlying meaning	Underlying meaning

From those experiences, what positive traits can you identify in yourself? In generally, how do you evaluate yourself from your responses to those events?

_____

_____

_____

Try to imagine 10 activities that can make you happy but you usually would not attempt to do (e.g., calling a good friend, doing exercise, or watching a movie).

Please rank these 10 activities by the extent of the pleasure they bring you and write them down on the right hand side of the Activity Ruler (the first one is the event that is 'the most easily achieved but low in the level of happiness', and the tenth one is the event that is 'more difficult to achieve but high in the level of happiness').

In the coming two weeks, which one would you choose to accomplish?

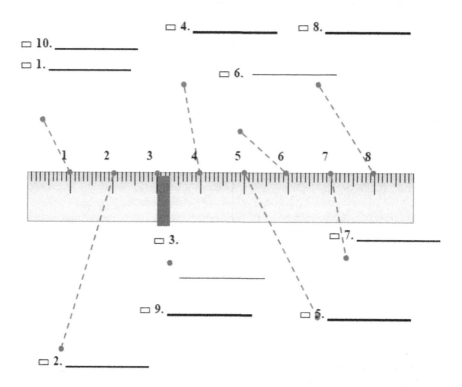

Try to use this worksheet to formulate your personal 5-Strategies.

Precipitating event

Negative thoughts
and
type of thought trap

Strategy 1	Strategy 2	Strategy 3	Strategy 4	Strategy 5
Aware of physical warning signals	Stop negative thoughts	Use self-talking technique	Use distraction	Use smart card

Worksheet 06 Costs and Benefits Analysis

1 Personal rule:

To what extent do you believe in this rule?

Yes, I believe .... Yes, I believe absolutely

1..........2..........3..........4..........5

Pros/helpfulness	Score	Cons/undesirable impact	Score

2 Rewritten / relaxed rule:

To what extent do you believe in this rule?

Yes, I believe .... Yes, I believe absolutely

1..........2..........3..........4..........5

Pros:	Cons:

Old Me:

Evidence:

1

2

3

New Me:

Evidence:

1

2

3

References

American Psychiatric Association. (2005). *Use of the concept of recovery: A position statement.* Retrieved from http://www.psych.org/edu/other_res/lib_archives/archives/200504.pdf

Andresen, R., Caputi, P., & Oades, L. (2006). Stages of recovery instrument: Development of a measure of recovery from serious mental illness. *Australian & New Zealand Journal of Psychiatry, 40*(11/12), 972–980. doi: 10.1111/j.1440-1614.2006.01921.x

Andresen, R., Oades, L. G., & Caputi, P. (2003). The experience of recovery from schizophrenia: Towards an empirically validated stage model. *Australian and New Zealand Journal of Psychiatry, 37,* 586–594.

Anthony, W. A. (1993). Recovery from mental illness: The guiding vision of the mental health service system in the 1990s. *Psychosocial Rehabilitation Journal, 16*(4), 11–23.

Beck, J. (2011). *Cognitive behaviour therapy: Basic and beyond.* New York: Gilford Press.

Campbell-Orde, T., Chamberlin, J., Carpenter, J., & Leff, H. S. (2005). *Measuring the promise: A Compendium of Recovery Measures* (Vol. II). Cambridge, MA: The Evaluation Centre @ HSRI.

Center for Mental Health Services. (2005). *National consensus statement on mental health recovery (Publ. No. SMA05-4129) [Brochure].* Rockville, MD: Substance Abuse and Mental Health Services Administration, US Department of Health and Human Services.

Clarke, S. P., Oades, L. G., Crowe, T. P., Caputi, P., & Deane, F. P. (2009). The role of symptom distress and goal attainment in promoting aspects of psychological recovery for consumers with enduring mental illness. *Journal of Mental Health, 18*(5), 389–397.

Cohen, J. (1988). *Statistical power analysis for the behavioral sciences* (2nd ed.). Hillsdale, NJ: Lawrence Erlbaum Associates.

Department of Health, State of Victoria. (2011). *Framework for recovery-oriented practice.* Retrieved from https://www2.health.vic.gov.au/getfile

Department of Health of Australian Government. (2010). *Principles of recovery oriented mental health practice.* Retrieved from http://www.health.gov.au/internet/publications/publishing.nsf/Content/mental-pubs-i-nongov-toc~mental-pubs-i-nongov-pri

Department of Health of Australian Government. (2016). *Fifth national mental health plan.* Retrieved from http://www.health.gov.au/internet/main/publishing.nsf/content/mental-fifth-national-mental-health-plan

Farkas, M., Gagne, C., Anthony, W., & Chamberlin, J. (2005). Implementing recovery oriented evidence based programs: Identifying the critical dimensions. *Community Mental Health Journal, 41*(2), 141–158.

Grant, P., Bredemeier, K., & Beck, A. (2017). Six-month follow-up of recovery-oriented cognitive therapy for low-functioning individuals with schizophrenia. *Psychiatric Services, 68*(10), 997–1002.

Grant, P., Huh, G., Perivoliotis, D., Stolar, N., & Beck, A. (2012). Randomized trial to evaluate the efficacy of cognitive therapy for low-functioning patients with schizophrenia. *Archives of General Psychiatry, 69*(2), 121–127. doi: 10.1001

Hansson, L. (2006). Determinants of quality of life in people with severe mental illness. *Acta Psychiatrica Scandinavica, 133*, 46–50.

Ho, S. M., Ho, J. W., Bonanno, G. A., Chu, A. T., & Chan, E. M. (2010). Hopefulness predicts resilience after hereditary colorectal cancer genetic testing: A prospective outcome trajectories study. *BMC Cancer, 10*(1), 279.

Hodgekins, J., & Fowler, D. (2010). CBT and recovery from psychosis in the ISREP trial: Mediating effects of hope and positive beliefs on activity. *Psychiatric Services, 61*, 321–324.

Hogan, M. F., Adams, J., & Arrendondo, R. (2003). *Achieving the promise: Transforming mental health care in America.* Rockville, MD: New Freedom Commission on Mental Health.

Ibrahim, N., Michail, M., & Callaghan, P. (2014). The strengths based approach as a service delivery model for severe mental illness: A meta-analysis of clinical trials. *BMC Psychiatry, 14*, 243. doi: 10.1186/s12888-014-0243-6

Jacobson, N., & Greenley, D. (2001). What is recovery? A conceptual model and explication. *Psychiatric Services, 52*(4), 482–485.

Jones-Smith, E. (2014). *Strengths-based therapy: Connecting theory, practice and skills.* New York: SAGE Publications, Inc.

Kisthardt, W. (2006). The opportunities and challenges of strengths-based, person-centered practice. In D. Saleebey (Ed.), *The strengths perspective in social in work practice.* New York: Longman.

Leamy, M., Bird, V., Le Boutillier, C., Williams, J., & Slade, M. (2011). Conceptual framework for personal recovery in mental health: Systematic review and narrative synthesis. *The British Journal of Psychiatry, 199*(6), 445–452.

Leung, K. F., Wong, W. W., Tay, M. S. M., Chu, M. M. L., & Ng, S. S. W. (2005). Development and validation of the interview version of the Hong Kong Chinese WHOQOL-BREF. *Quality of Life Research, 14*, 1413–1419.

Mak, W. W. S., Chan, R. C. H., Pang, I. H. Y., Chung, N. Y. L., Yau, S. S. W., & Tang, J. P. S. (2016). Effectiveness of wellness recovery action planning (WRAP) for Chinese in Hong Kong. *American Journal of Psychiatric Rehabilitation, 19*(3), 235–251. doi: 10.1080/15487768.2016.1197859

Marshall, S. L., Crowe, T. P., Oades, L. G., Deane, F. F., & Kavanagh, D. J. (2009). A review of consumer involvement in evaluations of case management: Consistency with a recovery paradigm. *Psychiatric Services, 58*, 396–401.

National Institute for Mental Health in England. (2005). *NIMHE Guiding Statement on Recovery.* Retrieved February 13, 2017, from https://manchester.rl.talis.com/items/1462D9CA-3228-11C7-CA3F-429526E1FC79.html

Oades, L., Deane, F., Crowe, T., Lambert, W. G., Kavanagh, D., & Lloyd, C. (2005). Collaborative recovery: An integrative model for working with individuals who experience chronic and recurring mental illness. *Australasian Psychiatry, 13*(3), 279–284.

Oades, L. G., & Anderson, J. (2012). Recovery in Australia: Marshalling strengths and living values. *International Review of Psychiatry, 24*(1), 5–10.

O'Hagan, M. (2004). Guest editorial: Recovery in New Zealand: Lessons for Australia? *Australian e-journal for the Advancement of Mental Health, 3*(1), 5–7.

Orde, T. C., Chamberlin, J., Carpenter, J., & Leff, H. S. (2005). *Measuring the promise: A compendium of recovery measures.* Cambridge, MA: The Evaluation Center @ HSRI.

Padesky, C. A., & Mooney, K. A. (2012). Strengths-based cognitive-behaviour therapy: A four-step model to build resilience. *Clinical Psychology and Psychotherapy, 19*(4), 283–290.

Rapp C, & Goscha R. (2012). *The strengths model: Case management with people with psychiatric disabilities* (3rd ed.). New York: Oxford University Press.

Rapp, C., & Goscha, R. (2014). *Strengths model: A recovery-oriented approach to mental health service core training manual [Brochure].* Melbourne, Australia: St Vincent's Mental Health.

Slade, M. (2009). Differences between traditional and recovery-oriented services. In M. Slade (Ed.), *100 ways to support recovery: A guide for mental health professionals.* London: Rethink.

Slade, M., Amering, M., Farkas, M., Hamilton, B., O'Hagan, M., Panther, G., … Whitley, R. (2014). Uses and abuses of recovery: Implementing recovery-oriented practices in mental health services. *World Psychiatry, 13*, 12–20.

Snyder, C. R., Harris, C., Anderson, J. R., Holleran, S. A., Irving, L. M., Sigmon, S. T., … Harney, P. (1991). The will and the ways: Development and validation of an individual-differences measure of hope. *Journal of Personality and Social Psychology, 60*, 570–585.

Substance Abuse and Mental Health Services Administration (SAMHSA) of the United States Department of Health and Human Services. *National consensus statement on mental health recovery.* Retrieved from http://www.samhsa.gov

Torrey, W. C., Rapp, C. A., Van Tosh, I., McNabb, C. R., & Ralph, R. O. (2005). Recovery principles and evidenced-based practice: Essential ingredients of service improvement. *Community Mental Health Journal, 41*, 91–100.

Tse, S., Cheung, E., Kan, A., Ng, R., & Yau, S. (2012). Recovery in Hong Kong: Service user participation in mental health services. *International Review of Psychiatry, 24*, 40–47.

Tse, S., Siu, B. W., & Kan, A. (2013). Can recovery-oriented mental health services be created in Hong Kong? Struggles and strategies. *Administration and Policy in Mental Health, 40,* 155–158.

Tse, S., Tsoi, E. W., Hamilton, B., O'Hagan, M., Shepherd, G., Slade, M., … & Petrakis, M. (2016). Uses of strength-based interventions for people with serious mental illness: A critical review. *International Journal of Social Psychiatry, 62*(3), 281–291.

Turkington, D., Munetz, M., Pelton, J., Montesano, V., Sivec, H., Nausheen, B., & Kingdon D. (2014). High-yield cognitive behavioral techniques for psychosis delivered by case managers to their clients with persistent psychotic symptoms: An exploratory trial. *The Journal of Nervous and Mental Disease, 202*, 30–34.

Wing, J. K. (1981). *Handbook of psychiatric rehabilitation practice.* Oxford University Press.

Ye, S., Pan, J. Y., Wong, D. F. K., & Bola, J. R. (2013). Cross-validation of mental health recovery measures in a Hong Kong Chinese sample. *Research on Social Work Practice, 23*, 311–325.

Young, S. L., & Bullock, W. A. (2005). Mental health recovery measure (MHRM). In Campbell-Orde, T., Chamberlin, J., Carpenter, J., & Leff, H. S. (Ed.), *Measuring the promise: A compendium of recovery measures (Vol. II)*, 36–41. Cambridge, MA: The Evaluation Center @ HSRI.

Zhang, W., Li, Y., Yeh, H., Wong, S., & Zhao, Y. (2007). *The effectiveness of the mental health recovery (including Wellness Recovery Action Planning) programme with Chinese consumers*. Hong Kong: Bo Ai She. Retrieved from http://www.tepou.co.nz/assets/images/content/your_stories/files/story011-4.pdf

黃富強, 李鳳葵, & 鄭燕萍 (Eds.). (2013). 家長情緒管理: 認知行為介入法的理論及應用. Hong Kong: City University of HK Press.

Index

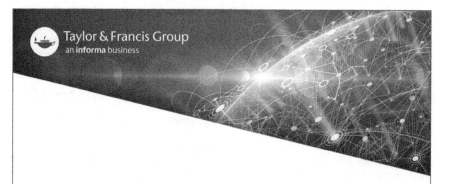

Made in the USA
Middletown, DE
21 August 2024

59536234R00104